BITS 'N' PIECES OF MY HEART

Colleen E. Peterson

LCCN: 2025940935

PREFACE

There are so many books published today by child psychologists, doctors, teachers, pastors, and others who are classified as experts. I am not an expert! I am a mother of two precious children. God gave their father and me two beautiful gifts, and allowed us to bring them into this world. When I began this book, Taryn (pronounced Karen, with a "T") was five years old, and Heather was three. Since their daddy, John, was a Minister of Music and Youth, I was often a mother, aunt, sister, friend, chaperone, confidante and counselor to twenty-five or thirty teen-agers. I knew I still had much to learn, but I also knew that I had a great deal to share.

God is always my strength and my resource to be a better mother. He has given me special thoughts, ideas, and insights to make preschool and childhood years with our children more meaningful and precious. It doesn't matter whether you are a full-time mother and homemaker, or a mother who works outside the home. I hope you use these God inspired "bits 'n' pieces" of my heart as little or as often as your schedule allows. The important thing is, no matter how short the time you have to spend with your children, you can make it special.

As I said, God is my resource. He is also my source. Everything I write has been given to me by Him. His Word says that if any of us lacks wisdom, we should ask for it. I believe He wants me to share His wisdom with you and others. So, I share with you experiences, ideas, songs and love . . . BITS 'N' PIECES OF MY HEART.

DEDICATED TO

Taryn and Heather, you are my beautiful and precious daughters. You are my inspiration, and I love you with all of my heart.

John, Taryn, and Heather's father, who they lost too soon. He was a father who loved his daughters dearly.

Richard, my husband, who is Taryn and Heather's stepfather. He loves and cares deeply for them each day.

Thank you,

Colleen

AUTHOR'S BIO

Colleen Peterson was born and grew up on the beautiful eastern shore of Maryland. As an adult, she has had the opportunity to live in Florida, Virginia and Ohio. She has a background of working with developmentally challenged teenagers and young adults within a county facility. Some of her activities at church included directing children's choirs, assisting with youth groups, and teaching puppeteering. She has also taught in Sunday School classes for different age groups. She was employed as a Human Resource Analyst for more than twenty years for the state of Ohio. Her daily goal is to interact with all people no matter what their ages. She loves sharing God's joy and happiness wherever she goes.

DESCRIPTION

First, being Christian-based, BITS 'N' PIECES OF MY HEART was inspired by the Scriptures and the love of God through Jesus. Second, being a mother of two beautiful daughters, inspiration came from each of them the moment they were born.

This book is just that! Everything you read here is a God-given piece of love from my heart. It's for parents, grandparents, and other family members to share with all the children in your family. If your precious child was just born, or is in the sixth grade, or anywhere in between, there are special ideas in the book just for them. It can be used in so many different ways as your child grows through all this time in his or her life.

BITS 'N' PIECES OF MY HEART contains stories, devotions and poetry for the adults, activities to do with your children, and fun little songs. The devotions and poetry will strongly open up your faith walk to more of God's light. Doing the fun activities and singing little songs with your children will bring smiles to everyone's heart.

Colleen

Stories

TOO YOUNG TO PRAY?

"Jesa . . . Bible . . . T'ank You . . . Wuv You . . . Bye . . . OK?" Could this brief, choppy sentence of a prayer be accepted or even heard by the Savior of this world? Does it mean anything to the God of all creation? In my mind and heart, I heard Jesus saying, "Yes, my dear child, I hear this beautiful prayer." As I thought about Taryn's prayer, it made me feel so happy to know that God had heard it. I heard Him responding to my young daughter in this way, "Yes, my child, I am listening to your prayer. It is filled with praise to Me and thanksgiving for all things. It is a beautiful prayer of confession and love with a cry for acceptance and guidance. Dear child, thank you for coming to talk to Me. Your prayer means so much to Me."

John looked at me from across the dinner table and confessed, "You know, I really wasn't sure she would respond when you started praying with her."

I felt as if this was something God wanted me to do with Taryn. Some people might think she was a bit young for praying since she would not be two years old for another four months. Still, I sensed a need to share quiet moments of prayer before bedtime with my little girl. I wanted her to feel my love and the boundless love that God has for her. I couldn't find any better way to communicate that love than by teaching her how to pray. As John and I talked more and more about it, we both decided the time was just right for her to get to know Jesus and talk to God as her friend.

Taryn has been going to church ever since she was two weeks old. A cold, November morning was the first occasion of her regular church attendance. She attends most Sunday mornings, Sunday evenings, Wednesday evenings, and many special occasions. The special times include extra choir rehearsals, spaghetti dinners, and meetings of every kind.

I'm not sure she could technically be called a "PK" (Preacher's Kid) because her dad is not a preacher. He is a minister of music and youth. Still, with the time spent in the church, I think she could qualify for the title of PK! For example, the first youth retreat that she attended was held about the time she had reached the ripe old age of two months. Later, at eight months old, she went to music week at the state Baptist camp.

In Taryn's two years, minus four months, she has lived in four different houses in two states. She has attended several churches and has traveled more miles by car and plane than most adults! She is quite experienced in meeting and dealing with new people. Exposure to so many different people in the church community has encouraged her lively, outgoing personality. She loves everyone, and they love her right back. With all the attention and popularity, she's received in her busy life in the ministry, I wanted her to begin to understand the real reason for what she was doing.

Singing and reading have always been an important part of our interaction with Taryn. I started singing "Jesus Loves Me" as soon as we brought her home from the hospital. Taryn has looked at books and listened to short stories since she was six months old. Her interest in books has increased as she has grown. As a result, she is familiar with songs and stories with the name of Jesus in them. We felt that it was about time for her to see that He was a real, living person with whom she could communicate and share her feelings. We started by looking for pictures of Jesus, be it on Granny's Bible, in her church nursery, at a bookstore, or any library. Taryn could see that Jesus was a man who held children like her on His lap, and He hugged them just like her Daddy did. He was the man who touched the woman who was "hurtin", and made her "all bettur". He would stand up "in dat boat" and talk to the people so everyone could hear what He had to say. I told her that Jesus loved her unconditionally, all of her friends, and everybody else. Through the words Taryn expressed as she looked at the pictures, I could already see a growing, loving relationship beginning to develop with the person she called Jesa.

The first night we prayed, I did the praying. Her eyes were blurred with sleep, but she looked up from the pillow and listened as I prayed. "Jesus, be with Taryn's Mommy and Daddy, and Grandma and Granddaddy, and Granny. Help Taryn to mind her parents. I love you, Jesus. Amen." The following night, I invited Taryn to talk to Jesus with me. When she got up on her elbows and said, "OK, Mommy, I want to!" tears sprang to my eyes. Her eagerness to pray made me realize how much God wants that communication with all of His children.

Taryn and I had been praying together, with me doing most of the talking for about a week. Since John was working a second job for a while, he did not have a chance to share this special time with us. I told him what we were doing and how Taryn was beginning to pray with me. "I wish I could be in on our family prayer time," he said wistfully. I appreciated John's support and enthusiasm for what we were doing, even though he could not be with us.

The first night John was free, Taryn was particularly cranky. She didn't want to go to bed at all, as usual, and she demonstrated her feelings with quite a noisy protest. Still, her father would not take "No" for an answer and carried her off to bed as I quietly followed. As he pulled her favorite blankie up, she must have decided to give in. Maybe she was finally beginning to realize that bedtime was something that came to every little girl, no matter how much she fussed! She tried to rub away the tears with her fist as she laid her head down on the pillow. I bent over the railing on her bed and whispered, "Taryn, let's pray to Jesus." Almost instantly, she closed her eyes and started to pray. Her voice was soft and sincere as she ended the brief prayer by saying "tank you" for the "ice ceam" she had that day! When we finished praying and kissed her goodnight, we left the quiet room. As I closed the door, I turned to see a proud father. "That was beautiful," he whispered. "She's really communicating with the Lord."

Since that night, John and I have continued to guide our little girl in her prayers. Sometimes, she will have more to say than others. Sometimes it is difficult for us to keep the grins from creeping across our faces as she honestly talks to God in her own childlike way. We encourage her to pray by suggestions and reminders; then she fills in the rest and ends her prayer as she desires.

The first time, she ended her prayer with a quick "OK, bye," I could not keep from smiling. But, when she looked at me and asked, "Funny, Mommy?" I knew how important our reactions were to her. I had to assure her that she had said just what Jesus wanted her to say. This experience reminded me that God knows what we are thinking, whether we say it or not. We cannot fool Him by trying to cover up our true thoughts and feelings.

As Taryn grows, so does her prayer life. It has become more of a daily attitude, rather than something we do only at bedtime and mealtime. It is not unusual for her to run up to me with a hurt finger and say, "Mommy, let's ask Jesa to make it feel bettur". She is learning that the good things in her life come from God, as we thank Him for the fun we had in the park or during a day at the ocean. She is also becoming aware of God's forgiveness when she tells Him she is sorry for not minding her daddy. Every time Taryn stops in the midst of her busy day to "talk to Jesa," she grows a little more in her relationship with Him.

The expressions Taryn comes up with continue to astonish us each time we talk about Jesus and pray with her. She seems to know that she should be more quiet and reverent in her own way. We notice that her voice becomes very quiet and soft, and her head is always bowed down. The words are never elaborate, and the sentences are not complete, as yet. But, the attitude of prayer is there. Taryn talks to Jesus in a beautifully, simple way that I hope will continue as she grows in her knowledge of God. She has shown us that we're never too old to learn from her, and she is not too young to pray.

BEST FRIENDS

Missy was a pretty doll who lived in the big white house on the corner. She had a soft pink face and golden ponytails tied with pretty pink bows. Her ruffled bonnet and dress were covered with pink flowers. She was just soft and cuddly enough to fit right under Heather's arm. Heather was the little girl who also lived in the big white house on the corner.

Ever since the first day Heather's Daddy brought Missy to live in their house, they had been very close friends. It was on her birthday, so she would never forget that special day. After that, Heather never went anywhere without Missy, her very best friend. She was always right beside her. When she took a bath, Missy waited for Heather on her own step stool. She was with her when her Mommy took her shopping. She always played with Heather in her bedroom, where all of the toys and games were. Heather and Missy were always together.

Heather loved to pretend she was cooking on her wooden stove. She planned tea parties and dinners for all of her friends. There were sandwiches and cakes to be made and cookies to decorate. The table had to be set just right. Missy always helped with the plans from the rocking chair where she sat. All of Heather's friends liked to come to the tea parties at Heather's house. Missy even became friends with all of them.

Missy even went along with Heather to places that were not always such fun. The doctor's office was one of those places. Even though it wasn't always fun, Heather knew she had to go. Sometimes, it helped to have a friend like Missy around when it was time for a shot. When Missy was there to hold her hand and keep her company, it didn't hurt so badly.

Missy's favorite part of the day was bedtime. After Heather finished saying her prayers, her Mommy and Daddy kissed her goodnight and tucked them in. Missy felt so snug and happy tucked under Heather's arm, with the warm blankets around them.

One beautiful Saturday afternoon, Heather and her Mommy took Missy to play in the park. The sky was so blue, and the grass was so green. It was the best way to spend the day. Missy sat on Heather's lap while her Mommy pushed them high in the swing. As they went up so high, she thought they would fly away with the birds. Next, they rode on the merry-go-round and then on the teeter-totter. Heather sat Missy under the big oak tree so she could watch her climb on the bars. She climbed and swung on the bars until she heard the tinkling bell of the ice cream truck. Heather and her Mommy skipped to where the truck was parked and ordered two double-dip chocolate cones. They decided it was time to go home to tell Daddy about all the fun they had at the park.

Back at the oak tree, Missy sat with tears rolling down her cheeks. She had watched as Heather and her Mommy skipped over to the ice cream truck. Surely, they would come back to get her before they went home. They just couldn't forget her.

Before she knew it, the sky began to grow dark around her. Missy watched as the stars popped out, one by one. She listened as the crickets chirped close by. Missy tried calling to the man she saw locking the park gate, but he didn't hear her. By now, she was shivering from the cool night air. She couldn't sleep in the park all night; she just couldn't! She missed being with Heather as she talked to Jesus in her prayers. Oh, where was Heather, she thought, as her sleepy eyes closed.

At home, Heather was getting ready for bed. She was happy, but she was tired from her busy day at the park. As she climbed into bed, she reached out to hold Missy. But Missy wasn't there! Where was she? She couldn't go to sleep without Missy. Heather and her

Mommy looked everywhere. They looked under her bed, behind the couch, and even in the car. Missy was just not there.

Then Heather remembered! She hadn't brought Missy in the house today when they returned from the park. Then she knew for sure! She had left Missy in the park by the oak tree.

Heather was heartbroken. The park was locked so they would have to wait until morning to find Missy. Heather tried hard to hold back the tears. If only Missy is still there tomorrow, I'll never forget her again. As she fell asleep, a tear rolled down her cheek.

The next morning, Heather rushed to get dressed. She tried to hurry through breakfast so she and her Mommy could be at the park when it opened. Just as they drove up to the park, the man opened the gate to visitors. Heather and her Mommy ran past the teeter-totter, the merry-go-round, and the bars to the oak tree. There was Missy! She was propped right where Heather had left her the day before. Missy was so happy to see Heather. She was very cold and a little wet from the morning dew, but Heather's arms felt nice and warm around her.

By bedtime that night, Missy was dry and warm. Her dress and bonnet were clean, and her ponytails were brushed. After Heather's Mommy and Daddy tucked them into bed, she listened to her say her prayers. Heather promised that she would never be careless with Missy again. They were both so happy to be warm and snug together with the blankets around them. As they fell asleep, they both had sweet smiles on their faces. It was so good for Missy to be home where she belonged.

THE BIGGEST AND BEST SNOWMAN

The morning sunlight peeked through the curtains of my bedroom window. It just wouldn't let me sleep, no matter how hard I tried. First one eye blinked, and then the other one opened. I heard bubbling and crackling sounds of yummy sausage frying in the kitchen. By now, bright beams of sunlight were pouring into my room, and I saw sweet, smoky swirls floating through the air. That could only mean one thing! It must have snowed last night! Mom always cooked sausage for breakfast when it snowed.

I had guessed right! When I looked out the window, I saw the world glittering and sparkling with piles of snow in the bright sunshine. The streets were crowded with children, padded and bundled up like little panda bears, racing their wooden sleds. Greeting visitors with their smiles, jolly snowmen already decorated many of the yards.

Quickly, I yanked my clothes on, splashed my face with cold water, and combed through my tangles. It seemed like I couldn't eat my delicious breakfast fast enough, but it finally disappeared from my plate. I ran to the closet and started piling on layers of warm clothes. On came extra fuzzy red stockings, a bright blue snowsuit, tall furry boots, warm mittens, and my favorite pompom hat. What a winter sight I was! The funny part was trying to get my arms and legs to move when I wanted them to. I must have looked like an astronaut in his space suit trying to walk on the moon.

As I stepped out into the deep snow, my play clothes seemed to disappear for a moment. I twirled around and around, feeling like a beautiful snow princess. The snow-covered neighborhood was my kingdom. Then SPLAT . . . My fantasy ended abruptly when a stray snowball hit me in the back. As I looked around, I saw two of the kids from down the block running away. Before I could roll up a snowball to retaliate, they were gone from sight.

In that instant, I decided now was the time for me to get busy. I was going to build the biggest and best snowman this whole town had ever seen! Rolling the three main sections was easy, but once that's done, you had to give your snowman a real personality. That took a lot of talent! Mine had a friendly face with brown moss eyebrows, blue stone eyes, and gray temples. He looked like a very handsome businessman in his brown hat, scarf, and shiny black buttons. All he needed was a briefcase and a cane from the trunk in the attic, and he would be ready for a hard day at the office. As I stood back to admire my good work, I heard Mom call me for lunch.

The vegetable soup and yummy hot chocolate helped bring the warmth back into my numb fingers and cheeks. I sat by the fireplace while I ate and looked out the picture window at my awesome "Mr. Snow." How tall and proud he stood, watching the people in the neighborhood come and go. I could have sat there all afternoon if I hadn't been so sleepy. It was so warm and cozy as I walked over to the couch and laid my head on the soft pillows. I felt my eyes blink a few times, trying to fight off sleep, and then they closed…

"Kathy, Kathy, wake up! Wake up!"

Oh, no, it can't be morning yet. I'm having such a nice time. I don't want to wake up yet. I was just a little girl like Susie. There was so much snow, and I built the nicest snowman, and…

"Kathy, Kathy, please wake up! It's snowing, Kathy! It's snowing! Mom's fixing sausage for breakfast. After we eat, we can go out and build a snowman in the front yard. Will you help me build a snowman, Kathy?"

"Oh, Susie, it's you! What did you say?"

"Kathy, it's snowing! I want you to help me build a snowman. Will you?"

When I realized what my little sister was saying, it all began to make sense. "Sure, Susie, I'll help you build a snowman! You know what, Susie?"

"What, Kathy?"

Suzie, we're going to build the biggest and best snowman this whole town has ever seen!"

Devotions

YEARS FULL OF LOVE AND SUNSHINE

You've heard it so many times before. You know it's true! The preschool and early elementary years of your children's lives are most important in setting the pattern for their later years. God has put you in the position to help form the person your child will grow to be. That time may seem to last forever, but don't blink twice! Before you've finished that second blink, you'll be watching them grow into young men and ladies. It doesn't seem possible, but it's so true!

Each of those preschool and childhood days holds a special place in my heart. You can spend them with the precious children God has given, and you can decide what those days will be like. They can be rocky, nerve-wracking, home-wrecking days. Or, with God, this can be a beautiful time of days filled with love and sunshine!! God has given every parent the job of training their children. He puts it plainly in Proverbs when He instructs us to "Train up a child in the way he should go, even when he is old he will not depart from it." As we attempt to carry out this training process in the way God intended, we grow as parents. Teaching, disciplining, and nurturing our children can be done successfully in an environment of joy and love. God's Word tells us so!

How can our home be filled with joy and love? Some folks may believe they have the ability to give their children all the love and training they need. You may be able to fake it on your own for a while, but without God, the true source of love and wisdom, it is impossible to be a successful parent. He must be the central, unifying force in your family.

Does God have that place in your home? It doesn't mean just going to church on Sunday and talking to Him there. God's Word, the Bible, teaches us what it does mean. Each parent needs to surrender the control of his or her life to the Lordship of Jesus Christ. We must realize that without Christ and what He did for us, we are sinners who are worthy of death. We must acknowledge that Christ paid the penalty for our sins when He died on the cross and then rose from the grave. By doing this, He has given eternal life to all who believe. Is this true in your life? If this is not the case in your home, you need to stop right now. Consider what Jesus Christ did when He obeyed His Father's will. He gave up His own life for you, and me, and everyone else. Please bow your head and your heart and ask forgiveness for your sins. Ask Jesus to be in complete control of your heart and life and to be your Lord and Savior. If you are already attending a church, ask for guidance in continuing service there. If you do not attend a church, ask for guidance to find one where you and your family can worship together and grow.

If you know for certain that both parents in your home have accepted Jesus Christ as their Lord and Savior, then take a moment to look closer. Is God the central, unifying force in your family? Is He being honored each day? Are you living for Him in all you do? Are you serving Him by giving Him your time and talents? Do your daily lives reflect His presence in the heart and life of you and your family? Are you seeking His love and wisdom to be a successful parent? If you can't answer "yes" to all of these questions, ask God to show you where to start. Listen carefully as He answers your prayer.

Am I saying our homes will be perfect? Of course, they will not. Our Lord knows we are imperfect, and that is why we will always need Him. My goal in our home is to have everything we do and say reflect and glorify the Lord Jesus Christ. That doesn't mean that every word we say must be a direct quote from the Bible. It doesn't mean that every waking moment is spent at church. It does mean that no matter what we do or say, we try to do it in a manner that will be pleasing to Christ and bring honor to Him.

I always enjoy listening outside the door of my daughters' playroom to hear them pretending.

"Let's get the babies dressed. We don't want to be late for church."

"OK. Don't forget your Bible. You need it for Sunday School." Sometimes, I would listen in on their pretend Sunday School class as they would begin. "Children, did you learn your Bible verse for today? Good, let's say it together, and then we'll sing our songs."

I think about some youngsters who are shooting at each other with make-believe guns or simulating a chase scene with the police that ends in a terrible crash. It is encouraging when your child's concept of life comes from a Christian home instead of the world. I'm not saying that church and Sunday School are their only pretend games. I also know that they are often far from the perfect little girls I would like them to be. They cannot spend their childhood years in a purified, plastic bubble that will ultimately burst when they walk into the real world. They need to be prepared to live in that world. That's why it is so important that I know most of what goes into their minds is based on Biblical principles. With that kind of background, and with God in control, they won't stray when they are older.

Have you paid attention to what your children are pretending to be? What games are they playing? Are they mommies and teachers, or are they detectives or girls living with their boyfriends? Are they going to a school, church, or sports activity, or are they shooting each other with guns or lasers from outer space? We do influence the direction our children's lives will take. As parents, God has given us the responsibility of raising our children according to His Word, not by the world's standards. Yet, we often let the world be our guide without even realizing it. As society's standards fall, ours have a tendency to be pulled down with them if we are not firmly holding on to Christ. What an awesome task we have been given! Still, it is up to us as Mommies and Daddies to train and mold our precious little ones into responsible adults. We can do this only with God's help! I believe this training process begins the first day your baby takes a breath in this world. Your love is conveyed to that baby in the way you touched her tiny hand or the way you softly sang in his ear. From that very first day until now, your precious child has grown in your care. As you continue to train this child, with God's help, make sure every day is beautiful and filled with love and sunshine!!

Bits of God's Wisdom in these devotions might bring verses from His Word to mind as you share these days with the gifts God has given you: your children.

WISDOM OF A CHILD

... And Jesus saith unto them, Yea: have ye never read, Out of the mouth of babes and sucklings thou hast perfected praise? (Matthew 21:16)

"Please, Mommy, please! Can we listen to our records? Heather and I want to listen to a record. We don't want to watch what's on TV. We want to listen to records!" As I flipped through the TV stations, Taryn was jumping up and down, pulling on my arm. Heather was following her lead. They were trying to persuade me to listen to their favorite records rather than watch TV. From songs they had learned in Sunday School, they both loved listening to and singing them.

There was no way I could refuse their pleading! They were learning the lesson I'd been trying to teach them. Today, they were teaching me! There are so many more interesting and fun things to do than watch TV all day. I realized Satan is using the television more and more in the world every day. It's become one of the main vehicles to share deception and trickery. The violence, suggestive language, actions, vanity, and other worldly issues we are shown can attack our families in very subtle ways. As these have eased themselves onto the screen and into our minds, we've found ourselves becoming used to them. We accept them without a fight. Things that would have upset us five or ten years ago are seen in homes every day without a thought.

God tells us to think on things that are honest, just, pure, lovely, and of good report. Our children must be brought up with this attitude instilled in their minds. To ignore what they watch on television is a tragic mistake. When we allow them to see cartoons or other shows filled with violence, hatred, magic, or witchcraft, we are falling short of the teaching in God's Word. If this garbage Satan is dumping on our children continually invades their minds, what effect will it have on them next week, next year, or five years from now?

What a precious reminder Taryn and Heather had given me! I praised God for the wisdom of my children as we sang the songs on their record that morning. They smiled back at me as we sang, "I am a promise. I am a possibility. I am a promise. I can be anything, anything God wants me to be."

Prayer

Dearest Jesus. You told the chief priests and scribes that God's praise would come out of the mouths of the children. This shows me one more way that Your Word is as appropriate for us today as it was when You walked on this earth. Thank You for our children. Help us not to forget the things they teach us every day. Help us realize how easily Satan can invade our homes by means of the television when we misuse it. Keep our eyes on You and our minds on things that are pure and lovely. We pray in the name of our Savior, Jesus Christ. Amen

RESPONSIBILITY FOR A LIFE

Train up a child in the way he should go, even when he is old he will not depart from it. (Proverbs 22:6)

The headlines read of child pornography, drugs, alcohol, depression, teen-age suicide, murder, abuse and much, much more! Sometimes, we might feel that if we don't read the newspapers or listen to news reports, we can forget those things are there. We would like them to go away. We would like to forget they exist. Unfortunately, we know they won't go away, and our hearts are sickened by that painful truth. How are these horrible realities affecting the lives of our precious children? They are not only in the high schools. You can find them in elementary schools, day care facilities, and on street corners everywhere. It breaks my heart to read of the young victims held in the clutches of such evils. More than that, it makes me angry!

The Word of God tells us to be angry and sin not! We should be angry at the evils around our children. These children are a gift from God, but the gift was not free. It came with a price tag of awesome responsibility. How foolish is the parent who takes that responsibility lightly. We are in a battle against Satan. If God is to control our children's lives when they become adults, we must train them as children. We cannot handle their lives as though they are nothing but toys or play things, and expect God to let us off without answering for it. Our children must be armed for battle by knowing God and His Word. Jesus defeated Satan in the wilderness by using Scripture, and we have the power to do the same! How can we allow our children to go out into this worldly battle unarmed? We must teach them what is right, and show them how to have the strength to stand up for it.

A dear friend of mine has shared something very special with me. She also wonders about the effects of the evils of this world on her children. She has always prayed for their lives each day. Since it has become a burden in her heart, she has started praying for their children's safe future before she goes to bed at night. She goes into their room after they're asleep, and places her hand on them as she prays. As you touch the child you brought into this world, how can you not feel the great responsibility to pray for their health, their school years, and their adult lives? *I challenge you to do this for your children!*

It takes an awesome commitment to be a parent; to pray for them at night, to teach them each day, and to live what you teach. Without that commitment, will your child become one of the statistics?

Prayer

Oh Father, help me feel the burden of responsibility for my children's lives. Help me to be faithful to pray and teach each one in the way they should go. Show me today where I've failed as a parent in the past. Forgive me when I take this position lightly. Help me to live a life that is consistent with what I teach. Father, use my children for Your glory, that Jesus may be seen in them. Amen

I DON'T WANT TO . . .

I delight to do Thy Will, O my God. (Psalms 40: 8)

Taryn is our resident bundle of excess energy. From the day she was born until now, her pattern has shown us that she is not a child who is fond of sleeping. She took only short catnaps for the first two years of her life. Finally, when she reached the ripe old age of two, she began to take a legitimate one or two-hour nap. That didn't mean she enjoyed it! It was usually just a matter of which of us was the most determined.

At the age of five, Taryn required a short nap only a few times a week. She was still very adamant in letting us know how she felt about the situation. "It's nap time" was, (and still is) a phrase which can bring on tears, stomping and pleading. No matter how sleepy she might be, she would never give in. She would rather cry to the bitter end, saying, "I don't want to take a nap." With that, her heavy eyelids usually closed in sleep. How often I had thought, if only I had time to take a nap today! I could fall asleep in two minutes flat. How about you? Do you have days like that?

Like Taryn, a typical energetic little girl, many of us rebel when God tries to tell us what's best for us. Sometimes, we may see that God is right, but we often say, "I don't want to, God!" He sometimes has to push and chasten us when we continue to rebel against His authority. As parents, we know when our children need rest, so we make them take a nap. It is often difficult to see past the pleading and the tears. Still, we tell our children that we know what is best for them, and we love them. Perhaps, we should listen to ourselves and realize God is saying the same thing to us. We can find out too late that our paths would have been smoother if we had done God's will in the first place.

Prayer

Dear Father, thank You for allowing me to be Your child. Please forgive my stubborn "I don't want to" attitude. Help me show my children what is best for them. Help me to realize that You know what is best for me. Let me delight in doing Your will today, and every day. Amen

ENJOY THEM NOW

Behold, children are a gift of the Lord. (Psalm 127:3)

"*They grow up so quickly. Enjoy your children now, while you can. Before you know it, they'll be all grown up!*" I'm sure most mothers have heard these statements from an older mother, grandmother or friend. They may seem to be overused clichés, but they've become true to so many. I remember every time, I fussed about a night without sleep, or a teething baby, someone would remind me that my babies would be growing up much faster than I would realize. As I look at my children now, at ages four and six, I am beginning to understand the wisdom of those words.

Not long ago, someone inquired about the ages of Taryn and Heather. After I had answered, I thought about the answer. It just didn't seem possible for them to be that old. Have you ever had those feelings? How has the time passed by so quickly, when it felt as if those days of diapers and bottles would never end? How could Taryn be going to kindergarten each morning? It seems like she's only been walking and talking for a little while. How could Heather be following on her sister's heels when it seems she was sleeping in a crib such a short time ago? Each question emphasizes more and more the importance of each day in our children's lives. We can miss so many special times by not being there to watch and take part in them. Even more heartbreaking are the times we are there with them, but we miss out because our minds are focused on a television show or other distractions.

I made a silent vow to experience as many precious moments as I could with my children. I wanted every day to be an occasion for celebrating little (but special) things. Affection and love need to be anytime, all the time occurrences. They say that adults need to be hugged and told that they are loved at least once a day. How much more do our children need that attention, support and love? I can't say that I've been the mother I want to be one hundred per cent of the time, but I'm trying!

We can't stop the days from passing, or keep our children from growing up. We can be there every day to share and experience their lives. We can love them and teach them in the way they should go. We can enjoy them, with all the struggles and joys and sorrows along the way. When we do look back, perhaps the time won't seem to be as much of a blur of years gone by. *"They grow up so quickly. Enjoy your children now, while you can. Before you know it, they'll be all grown up!"*

Prayer

Father God, Abba, Daddy, help us to use every moment of every day with our children. Allow us to look back on their childhood and know that we didn't miss out on those important moments because we were distracted. Thank You again for the gifts You give through them. Amen

COULD THIS BE WHAT HE MEANT?

Consider it all joy, my brethren, when you encounter various trials, knowing that the testing of your faith produces endurance. (James: 1:2, 3)

A sugar bowl (FULL OF SUGAR), a half-gallon of milk, a bottle of grape juice, and a broken glass . . . Who would believe all these ordinary kitchen items could land on our kitchen floor in only one-half hour? I can! Anything is possible in my kitchen. (Is it only in mine, or do things like this happen in yours?) This particular morning, all those things found their way to the floor by the extraordinary hands of a curious two-year-old.

No matter how well you train your child in the proverbial "no-nos", you're sure to experience a few days like this. As I picked up the broken glass, and the sugar ground under my shoes, I could feel my teeth grinding too! Surely, this cannot be what James meant. When he wrote, "count it all joy", he probably had never encountered a mess like this to clean up, while the phone was ringing off the hook, and the baby was crying. Huh, I thought! What does he know about the joys of a day like this?

Somehow, in the middle of that mess, God started to get through to me. On my knees, on the kitchen floor, I felt my anger subside, as I remembered the next few verses. I had been asking the Lord to give me patience, not realizing that trials were the very things that would produce the patience I requested. A mess, such as the one all around me, was just what I had prayed for! I felt God's presence right there as I confessed my sin, prayed for forgiveness, and thanked Him for answering my prayer for patience. I'll never forget the important lesson I learned that hectic morning. Truly, God does answer our prayers, but sometimes He definitely does so in a way we might not expect!

If you're a mother, you have probably had a day or two (or many more) like this one. You've probably asked God to give you patience at one time or another. Your trial may have been a dozen broken eggs on a freshly mopped floor or a pan of burnt gravy, just in time for your dinner guests. The principle is still the same. As I think of my trials, in comparison to the pain and suffering my Jesus endured, my heart breaks. Without our trials, we would never have an opportunity to grow, as difficult as that may seem. Without those opportunities to grow, we can become stagnant and feel worthless to ourselves, to others and especially to God. "Count it all joy . . ."

Prayer

Father, thank You for the big and the little spills in my life. Help me to realize that You work through those trials to make me more like Jesus. Forgive me when I react with anger and frustration, instead of praising You as You have told me to do. Remind me of those who are truly suffering. Remind me most of all of how Jesus suffered for me. Let me remember the next time I face one of those situations, to count it all joy. In the precious name of Jesus, I pray. Amen.

GIVE FEAR TO HIM

For God hath not given us the spirit of fear, but of power, and of love, and of a sound mind. (II Timothy 1:7)

It was a gorgeous summer day. John had brought a group of youth from our church to spend the afternoon at the beach. Several mothers, who were also close friends of ours, came along to help. We all brought our own younger children as well, to enjoy the cook-out and fun in the sand and sun.

I've always been a little uneasy about having my children around the ocean. Living about ten minutes from the ocean front hasn't helped the situation at all. I think it's something I carried over from my mother, who was terrified of the water, whether it was a river, pond, ocean or pool. I also remember the time when I was a child that those rough waves kept knocking me down as I struggled to get up. That memory may have influenced my thinking a little, too!

The afternoon's activities were going smoothly, until someone asked where Billy was. He was one of the younger brothers who had come to the cook-out. As we looked around, a sense of panic quietly swept through the group. I ran to give the lifeguard a description of Billy, while the others looked in the water, and up and down the beach. While all this was happening, I kept watching our friend Sue, Billy's mother. She was quickly, but calmly walking from one person to another, asking if her son had come by there. That uneasy knot in the pit of my stomach was beginning to turn into a terrible sick feeling.

Our searching went on for another five minutes, which seemed like five hours. Then, we heard boys shouting! Some of them had walked back to check near the church bus. They found

Billy playing nearby. Sue scolded Billy for going off without telling her. Still, she was very relieved. I think it was difficult for her to be too tough on him! Later, when I told her how frightened I had been, she said that she was scared, but peaceful. She had given her children to God. At the moment we realized Billy was missing, she put him in His hands, and asked God to protect him. Whatever the outcome, she knew God loved Billy, and He was in control.

What a testimony Sue was to me that day! Every time I hear of child who is missing, taken while walking home from school or from their own backyard, I wonder how I would react. What about those children who are abused, kept in a closet without adequate food, or sold for child pornography? Terrible thoughts . . . Yes, but those kinds of things happen many times a day, all across our country!

I have to claim II Timothy 1:7, and keep it in my mouth, in my mind, and in my heart. It is one of the most precious promises from God that a mother can have. Satan would have parents crumble beneath the evil he devises to capture our children. God has promised that if we keep His Word in our hearts, we do not have to fear. God has given us power, and love and a sound mind. Claim His promises, and take them as your own. Put your children in God's care every day.

Prayer

Our Father, I confess that of my own strength, I am nothing. I confess my fears to You, knowing they are sin. I claim Your power, and love and sound mind. I ask You to give me the wisdom to use these to care for my family. Thank You for Your promises. Amen

WITNESS OF A CHILD

... And Jesus saith unto them, Yea; have ye never read, Out of the mouths of babes and sucklings thou hast perfected praise? (Matthew 21:16)

When we got married, we had no time for a real honeymoon trip. It was one of those situations with the wedding on Saturday, and college classes continuing on Monday. Finally, after three years of marriage, we were finally able to take a trip together, just the two of us. My mother, being the special "Granny" that she is, agreed to keep our girls for the nine days we would be gone.

The thought of leaving our children for so long was difficult for us. Still, we knew it would be good for all of us to have a little vacation. Since we were going to be away that long, it would be a wonderful opportunity for Granny to really get to know "her girls". I prayed that Taryn, who was four at the time, would especially be a witness to my family. She was always singing "Jesus Loves Me" or other choruses she'd learned in Sunday School. Often, she would pretend to be the teacher, and Heather, her little sister, would be her "class"!

When we returned from our beautiful trip, we were met with this account of what happened one special day. One of my mother's good friends, Don (who later became my stepfather) had taken Taryn to the store for some groceries. When they came out to the car after shopping, Don immediately saw that one of the tires was almost flat.

"Oh no, Taryn, the tire's almost flat! I hope we can make it home," he said in a worried voice.

Taryn looked up at him and responded quickly, with the greatest assurance in her voice. "Don't worry, Don. Jesus will take care of us!"

What a testimony! What faith! Jesus did take care of them. They returned home safely, and without a problem.

From that day, Don shared this experience with family and friends. To this day, he will refer to it in conversation. I don't think he will ever forget it. I know God answered my prayer. Taryn's attitude, assurance and faith in Jesus meant so much more than anything I could have ever said or done.

I continue to pray that our children will always have a strong faith and testimony to share. Their example of trust and faith in God is something we can follow.

Prayer

Father, You have promised that You would never leave us. Help us to remember and believe all of Your promises. Help us to believe with the simple faith of a little child. It is so beautiful for me to see how our children trust You and believe Your Word. May we be more trusting of Your continuous care, and may we share this trust with others. Help us to be witnesses for You, just as they are. Thank You for answered prayer, Jesus. Amen

FAMILY TIES

"How very good and pleasant it is when kindred live together in unity!" (Psalm 133:1)

Living close to parents, grandparents, siblings and other family members allows you to spend more time together. Sometimes you can live down the street, a couple miles away, or just an hour's drive. When this is the case, your family can have dinner with Grandma and Grandpa, attend church together, and get together for all kinds of fun activities. Unfortunately, there can be reasons that prevent this from happening. Mommy's or Daddy's job may require you to move to live in another town, or even a state far from where your family is. If this is your family's situation, special planning is often required to visit your relatives.

During most of the time after our girls were born, we found ourselves living in different states, far from where my immediate family lived. They lived on the beautiful eastern shore of Maryland. At the time, we were living in a very small town near the border between Florida and Georgia. It did take much thinking and talking before we decided that I would drive to Maryland with Taryn and Heather. Since it was October, we planned the trip so we would arrive in my home town on the day they celebrated Halloween with "Trick or Treating" for the children! We planned to arrive just after the time that children would be heading around in my mother's neighborhood.

We arrived at the perfect time. The beautiful sunset hung over the bridge that led into the town. Street lights were already helping guide the children and families walking in the neighborhood. My mother's house was a block from the bridge at the entrance of town. I parked the car around the corner so she wouldn't be able to see us from her doorstep.

The girls' Granny had been a floral designer for many, many years in her brother's flower shop. This was helpful when we chose costumes for them to wear. It also helped to know that pink and purple were Granny's favorite colors. Heather was an adorable flower! She had green pants on, and wore an extra-large green hoodie sweatshirt so the sleeves hung over her arms to make "leaves". I had painted a pretty pink and purple flower on cardboard with the perfect sized center to fit around her face. Taryn was inside a big box with a hole on the top and two sides for her head and arms to come out. We had covered the box in glittery gift wrap with pink and purple hearts. Since I had worked in my uncle's shop I was fortunate to learn some design skills. I was able to make a big purple bow to tie around the top of Taryn's head.

Our plan was to walk from our car to her yard at the other corner of the block. We walked quietly to the shrubs around the side of the house, and waited until there was no one on her sidewalk. As I hid behind a bush, but was close enough to hear, Taryn and Heather slowly walked by the front picture window to the sidewalk, and rang the doorbell. When the door opened, they smiled and sang "Trick or Treat"! Granny's eyes widened with love and excitement! To say they received some sweet treats would be an understatement. They received sweet, surprised "Oohs, Aahs, Hugs, Kisses, and much, much more". To say that her granddaughters and daughter surprised their Granny doesn't even come close.

I came out from behind the bushes and joined in the best, loving family celebration. The "Trick or Treat" surprise was the beginning of a special week-long visit with Granny. Words cannot begin to express the importance of our time with her.

Prayer

Thank You, dear Father, for the gift of family that You have given us. Please help us to love them in Your way. Help us to spend as much time with them as possible. Allow us to share Your love with them. In Jesus name. Amen

MOM AND DAD, TAKE TIME FOR YOURSELF!

I will hide thy word in my heart that I might not sin against thee. (Psalm 119:11)

It took five years of marriage and motherhood for me to realize that I shouldn't feel guilty for taking some time for myself. Oh, I'd read it in books about being a successful woman. In fact, I knew it was probably a great thing to do; at least it sounded good to me. Every once in a while, I would try to squeeze in five or ten minutes to myself to read or just daydream. Often, my husband would tell me to go to my room to get away from everything. The results were always the same. I became more patient with the children and more loving and understanding with my husband. Everything, in general, went much more smoothly! Why, then, did I feel guilty for those twenty or thirty minutes a day?

Every Woman's Magazine has published its share of articles about working mothers. They all could handle a nine-to-five professional job, take care of the house, and raise a family. All that was done with one hand! With the other hand, they played tennis or golf, looked like a model and baked the Christmas cookies!! It's easy to see why I might feel like I was cheating to take a five-minute coffee break from my daily schedule of housework and child raising.

Ultimately, the enemy is responsible for planting those thoughts of guilt in our minds. When our minds aren't filled with God's word, the enemy has a chance to promote his cause. There is the original source of my guilty feelings. How foolish I was! Perhaps you, too, have tried to be a super-mom (or dad), perfect homemaker, and everything else wrapped up in one. I've learned that the Bible tells us that even the one who was perfect took some time to be by himself to rest and pray. Jesus spent time with God every day. During that time, He talked to God, but He also listened to what His Father had to say. How can we be in God's will when we do not spend time talking and listening to our Heavenly Father?

Jesus would often go away from the crowds who followed after Him. He needed to rest and relax, for although He was God, He was also man. If the perfect Son of God required time of prayer, and mental and physical rest, obviously, we imperfect ones must need the same and more.

If you experience a twinge of guilt as you sit down for a quiet time of rest or fellowship with God, look to Jesus. That twinge did not come from Him. The world can remind you of the laundry that just has to be finished, or those dirty windows to be washed. Turn that twinge of guilt into praise. Tell the enemy to get out and ask Jesus to fill you afresh with His Spirit. Ask Him to guide you in scheduling your housework so things get done with time left for resting in Him.

Take time for yourself each day to become a better mother and a happier wife (or a better father and happier husband). Spend time daily communicating with God. Talk to Him. Tell Him your feelings, desires, fears, and hopes. Listen to Him speak to you as you read His Word. It will make a beautiful difference.

Prayer

God, help me to get my housework and other responsibilities on a schedule. Remind me that I need to stop each day to relax and rest. Help me to seek Your will when other things try to crowd out my time with You. Thank You for making me a woman (or man). Thank You in the name of Jesus, Your Son. Amen

LORD JESUS

Jesus,

Lord Jesus.

Yes, I can call You Lord.

By the Holy Spirit's power.

each precious day, and every hour,

I can call You Lord.

    The Bible reveals to us that only by the power of the Holy Spirit can we call Jesus Christ our Lord. If, by that power, we call him Lord, He wants us to allow Him to be Lord of our life. This is something He always wants; not just on Sunday morning, but every hour of every day. He wants to be the Lord of every precious hour we spend on this earth. Jesus wants us to know He's there, in control, at two a.m. as we rock our sick child. He is there as we mop up spilled grape juice from the new carpet, or wash muddy clothes. He knows these things are a part of our life. As we experience it all, the difficult and the easy times, we must let Him be in control of us. We can ask Him to be Lord through it all.

    What a privilege it is to know that we can have such a special, personal relationship with Jesus, our Lord. In fact, that is exactly what God wants and expects from us. Imagine, He wants to be the Lord of a housewife and mother. We aren't on a platform in the limelight. We are not the "star of the show" with fans crowding around and clamoring for an autograph. Still, we know that He wants to have a close relationship with each one of us who are His children. It's so nice to feel sure that we don't have to be someone different than the person God, our Father, has called us to be. If we would just do that, we would have our hands full. He's promised to love us, help us, be with us, and be the Lord of all we are and all we do. We only have to step aside and allow Him to be just that.

Sometimes, the stepping aside is the hardest thing we have to do. We do have our human side that makes us want to hold on. It tends to make us want to decide what we do with our life. We need to realize that God's plan is the best for us, and let Jesus take control of every situation, every day. As we do, we find our lives becoming more and more beautiful.

When you accepted Jesus Christ as your Savior, He should have also become your Lord. Have you allowed Him to be what He wants to be, what He should be? Who controls your daily activities, you or Jesus? If you call Him Lord, are you allowing Him to take that position?

Prayer

"Lord Jesus, I praise You and thank You for being my Savior and my Lord. Forgive me when my human nature takes control. Forgive me when I push You out of Your rightful position in my life. Help me to step aside and accept Your perfect guidance. Help me to allow You to be in control. Thank You for being there every hour of every day. Thank You for loving me that much. I love You, Lord. Amen

Poetry

PIECES OF POETRY FOR YOU

Mommies, Daddies, and Grandparents should strive to spend time reading God's Word, the Bible. Along with this, there are many books out there with daily devotionals to read with Bible verses and prayers.

These poems that I share are especially for parents, grandparents and families. Hopefully, they will allow you to think about certain situations you've had or will experience in the future. After reading some Bible verses (or anytime), you can read one of these poems. They are from experiences I've had, and they are a few more BITS 'N' PIECES OF MY HEART.

LITTLE CHILD

Little child, little child, sleeping in my arms . . .
You ran and played so hard today.
You bubble with such charm.
Little one, little one, so peaceful in my arms . . .
I love you more than I can say.
I pray you'll meet no harm.

I promised I would love you.
I made this vow to you.
The love I give remains unchanged.
No matter what you do!

Little child, little child, much like me today . . .
I ran and fell so hard today.
I tried it my own way.
Little one, little one, I hear the Father say . . .
I love you more than I can say.
I pray you'll walk My way.

I promised I would love you.
I made this vow to you.
The love I give remains unchanged.
No matter what you do!

Little child, little child, He is by our side . . .
We run and sometimes lose our way.
Still, He is there to guide.
Little one, little one, we never have to hide . . .
He loves us more than He can say.
We live because He died.

He promised He would love you.
He made this vow to you.
The love He gives remains unchanged.
No matter what we do!

A MOTHER

A mother changes diapers,
and rocks as sleep would fall.
She reads aloud
and chases giggling children down the hall.
For little girls, she takes the time
a tea party to plan.
And just for her own special boy,
she builds a house of sand.

She listens to them daily
when they come home from school.
She prays for them
and teaches them there always will be rules.
When questions come of life and love,
she shares what God's Word tells.
She leads and guides them to the Lord
and listens to them well.

She feels the pain they're feeling
in every fall they take.
She knows the joys,
the hurts, the fears in every move they make.
She plays with rattles, trucks and cars,
and dolls, and baseball gloves.
She watches as they grow each day,
and fills their lives with love.

She prays as they are sleeping,
for all their future days.
She prays their path
will follow God and from Him never stray.
A mother gives the life she has
for these gifts from above.
A mother is all this, but more…
a mother is pure love.

JOY IN THE DAY

Good morning Father, Abba, Daddy mine.
Thank you for such a beautiful day!
You've given blue skies, sunshine, oh so fine.
They make me want to share all You say!

As I walk with You down the street today,
You have filled my heart with joy that shows!
I want to praise and sing so others may
witness joy You give that overflows!

Heading back home from the park, I can feel,
the hand of the Lord leading my way!
It reminds of His love and presence real,
ev'ry minute of each lovely day!

Father, please continue to walk with me,
no matter what it is I may do!
So. people can look at me, and they see,
You're their Father, Abba, Daddy too!

IN THE MORNING

Let me arise in the morning,
just as the day becomes new.
Let me awake with new joy in my heart,
and give this day to You.
Let me arise in the morning,
just as the world starts to sing.
Let me awake with a song on my lips
to praise my Savior King!

Let me arise in the morning
and seek Your will and Your way.
Let me awake with Your love in my heart
to share with all today.
Let me arise in the morning,
just as sunshine floods my soul.
Let me awake with a smile on my lips.
Renew and make me whole!

Let me arise in the morning
and give thanks for this new day.
Let me awake with Your peace in my heart
to carry through the day.
Let me arise in the morning,
just as Your word fills my mind.
Let me awake with a prayer on my lips.
that Your will I will find.

HE'S PERFECT LOVE

Love, it was a man.
Love, it was God's plan.
Love brought Jesus Christ down to the earth.
Love, in human form, as a baby born,
Love brought Jesus Christ down to the earth.

Only He could leave His glory.
Only He could die.
Only He could pay the price I owe for all my sins.
He was the perfect Lamb,
our God's own perfect plan
Jesus Christ is love.
He's perfect love.

Love, it was a cross.
Love is what it cost.
Love raised Jesus Christ up from the grave.
Love was victory, won for you and me.
Love raised Jesus Christ up from the grave.

Only He could leave His glory.
Only He could die.
Only He could pay the price I owe for all my sins.
He was the perfect Lamb,
our God's own perfect plan
Jesus Christ is love.
He's perfect love.

Love is what I bring.
Love is Christ, my King.
Love will save your soul from death and hell.
Love, He is the way. Trust in Him today.
Love will save your soul from death and hell.

Only He could leave His glory.
Only He could die.
Only He could pay the price I owe for all my sins.
He was the perfect Lamb,
our God's own perfect plan
Jesus Christ is love.
He's perfect love.

JESUS LOVES YOU

Hey, you guys.
Won't you listen when we say?
We've got some awesome news,
and it's just for you today!

Jesus loves you.
This is true.
Yes, He cares no matter what you do.
Jesus loves you, and He'll change your life.
This is true.
He is there, and He will always help you through.

Hey there, world.
Don't you put it off too long.
We've got some awesome news,
and it just can't steer you wrong!

Jesus loves you.
This is true.
Yes, He cares no matter what you do.
Jesus loves you, and He'll change your life.
This is true.
He is there, and He will always help you through.

Hey, out there.
Don't you know that He loves you?
We've got some awesome news,
that He gave His life for you!

Jesus loves you.
This is true.
Yes, He cares no matter what you do.
Jesus loves you, and He'll change your life.
This is true.
He is there, and He will always help you through.

I WATCH YOU SLEEPING

I watch you sleeping,
so quiet and so small.
I watch you sleeping
without a care at all.

I see your sweet face,
so special and so dear.
I see your sweet face
and feel God's presence near.

I hear you breathing,
so gently and so true.
I hear you breathing
and know God hears you too.

Father, God,
I come to You
with all my heart in prayer.

Father, God,
I pray that You
give her all Your love and care.

Father, God,
I give my child
into Your precious love.
In the quiet of this hour
I pray You care for her each day.

Guide my child,
please fix and mold
a life pleasing to you.
Touch my child now in this hour
Bless her to serve You every day.

LITTLE ONES

. . . Permit the little children to come unto me, and forbid them not for of such is the kingdom of God. (Mark 10:14)

The children came to see the Lord.
His friends said, go away.
Then, Jesus turned and looked at them,
and He was heard to say . . .

Little ones, little ones.
Let them come.
Foolish men, don't you see.
Leave them alone.
To such as these, my kingdom belongs.
To hinder them is wrong.
Learn from the children.
Become as they:
Trusting Me, loving Me, in child-like faith.
They are a gift from Me.

Little ones, little ones.
I love them.
Precious ones, all their lives
wait on ahead.
Don't let them need things this world can share.
Just let them know you care.
Listen, My children.
Don't go away.
Stay with Me; learn of Me, more each new day.
You are a gift from Me.

Little ones, little ones.
Let them stay.
Precious ones, I give them,
My peace today.
Don't let them find answers others give.

They'll have no joy to live.
Give to the children
My love each day.
Share with them, teaching them more of God's way
They are a gift from Me.

A SIMPLE PLAN

A simple truth . . .

A simple plan . . .

God's perfect love became a man.

Wise men call it foolish.
They cannot understand,
but for those who will believe, it's God's salvation plan.
Clever words don't hold the key,
not works, not bargains made.
You simply must believe to live.
Your ransom has been paid.

Jesus. He died.
He shed His precious blood.
Jesus. He conquered death,
and reigns with God above.

Jesus' own disciples,
they could not understand.
but to those who will receive, He is the spotless lamb.
Turn from sin. Give Him control.
Repent, and be made whole.
You simply must believe to live,
for He's redeemed your soul.

Jesus. He died.
He shed His precious blood.
Jesus. He conquered death,
and reigns with God above.

A simple truth . . .

A simple plan . . .
God's perfect love became a man.

A SPECIAL GIFT!

A special gift arrived for us!
It came so quietly . . .
. . . perhaps you did not know.
There was no fancy wrapping,
not even a pretty bow,
no ornate frills or glitter,
no festive party mood . . .
. . . Just a tiny baby boy
born in a stable crude.
He was our Savior King.
He came to earth to bring
God's gift of love!

God's greatest gift was giv'n to us.
It was His only Son . . .
. . . perhaps you did not know.
He left a throne in heaven
to come to our world below.
His birth was without grandeur;
a star, His only crown;
. . . Just a precious little babe;
our God, to earth, came down.
He is our Savior, King
To Him, all Praises sing
God's gift, great love!

So, turn your eyes from the glitter,
of Santa's presents bright . . .
. . . perhaps you need to know.
Just turn from what the world sees,
and gaze on that glorious night.
Look there upon the baby
in God's own holy light.

. . . Now, look past the party crowds
past shopping to be done.
Look past all worldly things.
Look at the baby king,
God's Gift has come!

I SING

In my heart, I have a song.
I want to sing it all day long.
Sing of one who's mighty.
Sing of one who's strong.
Sing of one who loves me;
One I depend upon.
I sing of Jesus Christ, my Lord.
I sing of Jesus Christ!

He put His love within my heart.
He gave me His song to sing.
He is my Lord.
He is my God,
my Savior, and my King.
My song His message brings.
I sing of Jesus Christ!

In my heart, I have a gift.
I want to share it all day long.
Share of one who's mighty.
Share of one who's strong.
Share of one who loves me;
One I depend upon.
I share of Jesus Christ, my Lord.
I share of Jesus Christ!

He put His love within my heart.
He gave me His song to sing.
He is my Lord.
He is my God,
my Savior, and my King.
My song His message brings.
I sing of Jesus Christ!

ONLY GRACE

Thank You, Jesus, for taking my place.
Father, thank You for Your precious grace.
You sent Your own Son to make a way,
for those yesterday and us today.

From Your Word, we learn, dear God,
that for us, Your grace is the only way.
We must believe Christ gave His own life
and that You raised Him to life that day.

No one can be good enough for You.
Good thoughts, good works just won't pull us through.
Only the sacrifice of Your Son
paid the price for sin that all have done.

From Your Word, we learn, dear God,
that for us, Your grace is the only way.
We must believe Christ gave His own life
and that You raised Him to life that day.

Help me, Father, to share Your good plan;
why You sent Jesus to live with man.
Believe and trust in what He has done.
Receive His salvation, everyone.

From your Word, we learn, dear God,
that for us, Your grace is the only way.
We must believe Christ gave His own life
and that You raised Him to life that day.

Help me, Father to share Your good news;
so others will put their trust in You.
Believe and ask to become His child,
And in God, through Christ, be reconciled.

From Your Word, we learn, dear God,
that for us, Your grace is the only way.
We must believe Christ gave His own life
and that You raised Him to life that day.

SPEAK TO YOUR CHILDREN, LORD SPEAK

As we humble ourselves now before You, dear Lord,
Speak to Your children, Lord speak.
As we turn from all the wicked ways of the world,
Speak to Your people, Lord speak.
Speak in a still, small voice.
Speak in our songs as we rejoice.
Speak through Your servant.
Speak in our prayers.
Lord, we know You are always there.
We bow now before You.
It's Your will we seek.
Speak to Your children, please speak.

As we wake up this morning to start our new day,
Speak to Your children, Lord speak.
As we head off to work now or spend time at play,
Speak to Your children, Lord speak.
Speak to us in our heart.
Speak through Your nature's work of art.
Speak through each hour.
Speak in our prayers.
Lord, we know You are always there.
We bow now before You.
It's Your will we seek.
Speak to Your children, please speak.

HOPE

In my pain, I found healing.
From dark sorrow came real peace.
To the struggles deep within me,
He brought His sweet release.
Despair was all around me when hope broke through!

Hope . . .
a new tomorrow.
Hope has filled my soul.
Christ . . .
my hope of glory.
Christ has made me whole.
He came to me in all my sins.
He brought new life and love.
I can begin again today with hope in God above.
Everywhere I look, I see people I must tell.
They are living in the darkness,
dying to an endless hell.

To this world, God sent Jesus.
Let me tell you what He's done.
He has given all His life's blood,
to be the only one.
He paid for all your sin, child, and brought you hope!

Hope . . .
a new tomorrow.
Hope has filled my soul.
Christ . . .
my hope of glory.
Christ has made me whole.
He came to me in all my sins.
He brought new life and love.
I can begin again today with hope in God above.
Everywhere I look, I see people I must tell.

They are living in the darkness,
dying to an endless hell.
Hope!

GIVE ME THE WORDS TO SAY

Lord, please give me the words to say,
To those who are lost along their way . . .
Lost on the road of sin,
Lost in the world that I was in,
before You saved my soul.

Help me tell that lonely girl, who has run away from home.
Fill my mouth with words of love,
And fill my heart with joy.
Move my arms to wrap the warmth of Your love 'round her now.
Don't let me question, or let me judge.
Don't let me walk away.
Give me words from Your own heart to share love with her now.

Help me share the love of God with a woman on our block.
Fill my mouth with words I need,
And let them flow with ease.
Move me past my timid shell to share love You give me.
Don't let me gossip or let me brag.
Don't let my tongue control.
Give me strength to tell her how You died to set us free.

Help me show to all the world in the things I do and say.
Teach me how to give control,
And let You lead the way.
Move my heart to break each time I see one in need, Lord.
Don't let me fail You, or let me stop.
Don't let my heart turn cold.
Give me love to show them how You died to save them, Lord.

Lord, please give me the words to say,
To those who are lost along their way . . .
Lost on the road of sin,
Lost in the world that I was in,
before You saved my soul.

ALWAYS

The explosion of the colors in a sunset
meets the starkness of the cold winter trees.
And a star that glows o'er the horizon just begins to say
what my God means to me.

Oh, He gave us a world,
a beautiful world.
You can see it in the mountains.
You can see it in the meadows.
It's there in a smile.
It's there for a while.

The explosion of the wreckage of a building
meets the hardness of a black, two-lane street.
And a sign that blinks outside a window, as it seems to say
what is man's need for me?

But God gave us the world,
a natural world.
You can see it in the seashells.
You can see it in a snowfall.
It's there in a cry.
It's there for a while.

The explosion of the colors in a sunset
paints a picture of harmony God gave.
And it's there to be just a reminder, when I lose my way,
that my God's always there.

Yes, He gave us a world,
this beautiful world.
You can see it in the flowers.
You can see it in the family.
It's there in each day.
It's there for always!

It's there in each day.
It's there for always!

My dad loved God, and he loved nature. Growing up near the Chesapeake Bay in Maryland, he enjoyed the beautiful world God created for us. He loved spending time in it. At the end of a life that was much too short, he was working in the Facilities Department of a state college. There, he was responsible for things such as building plans, blueprints, and construction contracts for the college. I wrote "Always" for him to be sung at his funeral.

A GIFT FROM YOUR MISSY AND THE CUTEST BEAR, FRED

We had a long chat, your Missy and I.
We did not agree, and let me say why!
She hemmed, and she hawed, and then she started to whine.
'bout some clothes, or some jewelry, or roses so fine.
I had to refuse all your Missy's poor tries.
I said, listen to me, a cute bear who's so wise!

A Mom is a gift; she's special for sure.
On that she agreed, so I told her more!
She works, and she loves, and she helps children to grow
in their hearts, and their values, and things they should know.
To honor the love, she has given so long,
I said, listen to me, a cute bear can't go wrong!

Just give from your heart, and let me explain.
This gift comes with love, that's simple and plain.
It's sent, just for you, this gift card, I do repeat.
So, relax, have your hair done, or pedicure neat.
She's saying she loves a Mom who is the best.
I say, listen to me, a cute bear must know best!

So, she was so smart and heard what I said.
So you can be sure, since I'm cute bear Fred!
I'm here, and I bring love from your Missy and me.
Here's a kiss, and a big hug, and a gift, you see,
to say that we both love you Mom on your day.
I'm here, listen to me, a cute bear, when I say . . .

We love You, Happy Mother's Day

COME LEARN

Come learn about the babe.
He came to earth, with man to dwell.
The shepherds came to give Him praise,
God's own Son, Emmanuel.
Come kneel beside the babe.
See where His life on earth began.
He came to save and make us new.
His birth brought new hope to man.

Come learn about the man.
His life on earth taught of God's love.
Disciples followed Him to find
real joy from our God above.
Come kneel before the man.
See how He holds you in His hand.
He came to save and make you new.
For each one, He has a plan.

Come learn about the Lord.
He sits beside His Father, there.
If you just give your life to Him
He'll keep you within His care.
Come kneel before the Lord,
and ask for guidance every day.
He gave His life to make you new,
and with you, He'll always stay.

IF YOU WOULD BELIEVE IN JESUS

If you would believe in Jesus,
He would take all your sins away.
If you'd only believe in Jesus,
Then, with you, He would stay.
Come now and let the Savior in.
Surrender all you have to Him.
Surrender all you have to Him.
He would take all your sins away.

Put your trust in God's own Son,
for He is the only way.
With Jesus Christ, the battle's won.
Sing praise, rejoice today!

If you would believe in Jesus,
He would love you and understand.
If you'd only believe in Jesus,
He'd be your closest friend.
Don't wait; just let the Lord come in.
Today's the day to follow Him.
Today's the day to follow Him.
He would love you and understand.

If you would believe in Jesus,
He would give you a song to sing.
If you'd only believe in Jesus,
abundant life He'd bring.
Just listen to the Spirit's voice
You have to make the final choice.
You have to make the final choice.
He would give you a song to sing.

Put your trust in God's own Son,
for He is the only way.
With Jesus Christ, the battle's won.
Sing praise, rejoice today!

If you would believe in Jesus . . .

KEEP YOUR EYES UPON JESUS

Day in and day out;
laughter or tears.
Problems and struggles;
held captive by fears.
If only life would go just as I had planned.
Life would be perfect, I'm sure.
I know then, that I could endure.

Year in and year out;
joy and success.
Triumphs and vict'ries;
we fight and win less.
If only I could reach the top of the hill,
Life would be special, I know.
I know then, the world I could show.

but broken . . .
. . . and shattered,
I fall in defeat!
Life doesn't go just as I had planned.
I cannot reach the top of the hill.

Then, my heart can remember some words I have heard . . .
Over and over again they repeat.

Keep your eyes upon Jesus.
He is forever.
Those times in your life are held in His care.
Keep your eyes on the Savior.
Give it all to Him.
Your life is His plan.
He will carry you.

Keep your eyes upon Jesus.
He is forever.
Those times in your life are held in His care.
Keep your eyes on the Savior.
Give it all to Him.
Your life is His plan.
He will carry you.

THINKING OUT LOUD!

It wasn't so long ago that I was in CONTROL.
My life was MINE alone.
At the time, it seemed the perfect way to live,
yet then
I
Had
No goal.

THEN CHAOS WAS MINE!

When problems came, I fell apart, in pain none could bear.
The ANGER often flared.
Many times, there was no joy within my world,
no one
Came
Near
To care.

LONLINESS WAS MINE!

A stranger came along and showed me a better way.
Just give GOD all CONTROL
On that day, surrender came into my heart
then His
Peace
Made
Me say.

VICTORY WAS MINE!

Now when problems come, I go to Him, my Savior and my Lord.
I follow Him each day I live.
Life's purpose He restored!
The rough days come, but now I know,
They're always in His hands.

I've found the perfect way to live
within God's special plan.

HIS OWN JOY IS MINE!

CAN THIS BE ALL THERE IS?

The air we breathe is dirty.
Our morals have decayed.
The home's no longer sturdy,
and parents are dismayed.
Children act like grown-ups . . .
. . . Some adults act like kids.
Time bombs wait to blow up.
Can this be all there is?
No!
No!
There's Jesus Christ!
His love will save you.
Put your faith in Jesus Christ
It's something you must do.

The lives we live seem empty,
although our days are full.
So many still go hungry,
while we fill tables full.
Drugs have taken over
the minds of many here.
Is the only answer,
to live our lives in fear?
No!
No!
There's Jesus Christ!
He can calm the storm.
Put your faith in Jesus Christ,
and you will be reborn.

In sin, the world devours us.
In sin, we find defeat.
We see the world's confusion,
in people that we meet.
Life is never easy,

and problems linger near.
Is the only answer
to live our lives in fear?
No!
No!
There's Jesus Christ!
His love makes you whole.
Put your faith in Jesus Christ.
His peace will fill your soul.

I DON'T NEED IT

Come on; anything goes.
Come and see; don't ya know.
Now is the time to live.
Now is the time to give
yourself a chance.
Come on and take a second glance,
at what this world has to offer you.

I don't need it.
I don't need it,
not anything that you've got.
I don't need your kind of fun,
or feelin' good;
not anything you've got.
I have abundant life,
real peace and joy within.
Mine's eternal life,
free from death and sin.

Come on; it's all for fun.
Worries cares; we've got none.
Now is the time to play.
Now is the time to say,
"I live for me".
Just try it and then you will see,
how great the things of this world can be

I don't need it.
I don't need it,
not anything that you say.
I don't need your party life
or easy out;
not any of your ways.
I have a better life
and have no need to stray.

Free from sin and strife,
with Jesus I stay.

Come on; it's all for fun.

I don't need it.

Come on; it's all for fun.

I don't need it.

I don't need it.

I have Jesus Christ!
Come seek Jesus Christ!

WE HAVE TO TELL EVERYBODY

He came to earth,
a baby boy.
He grew to be a man.
He taught us of the Father's love,
and His salvation plan.

We have to sing about it.
We have to talk about it.
We have to tell it, live it, share it.
We have to shout it!
We have to tell everybody of Jesus' love.

He gave His life,
for everyone.
He took on all our sins.
He died upon a cruel cross,
but death could never win.

We have to sing about it.
We have to talk about it.
We have to tell it, live it, share it.
We have to shout it!
We have to tell everybody of Jesus' love.

He rose again
and always lives
His victory we sing.
Because His life is now our own,
we serve our Savior King.

THIS IS NOT SOMETHING WE CAN CHOOSE.
WE MUST SHARE THIS SPECIAL NEWS.
JUST LIKE PETER, JOHN AND PAUL.
WE MUST TAKE THE NEWS TO ALL.

We have to sing about it.
We have to talk about it.
We have to tell it, live it, share it.
We have to shout it!
We have to tell everybody of Jesus' love.

JESUS MY SAVIOR, BECAUSE IT'S YOU

I can hear a raindrop.
I can feel the stillness.
I can see forever in the sky up above.
Music plays so softly . . .
and hearts are gently beating.
Moonlight falls around us as we're wrapped in God's love.

I don't hear the thunder.
I don't feel the wind blow.
I don't see beyond us, for You are by my side.
Quiet all around us . . .
and all the world is sleeping.
Nothing else compares to what I'm feeling inside.

Why?
Because every day is different.
Every day is precious.
Every day is special.
There's something so brand new.
No one else can save me.
No one else understands and listens.
No one else can love me just the way You do.
Why?
Jesus, My Savior, because it's You . . .
Jesus My Savior, because it's You . . .

I can hear Your voice now.
I can feel You near me.
I can see the heart of God's gentle, caring Son.
Music plays a sweet song
my faith grows even stronger.
God's love holds me closely in the vict'ry He's won.

Why?
Because every day is different.
Every day is precious.
Every day is special.
There's something so brand new.
No one else can save me.
No one else understands and listens.
No one else can love me just the way You do.
Why?

Jesus My Savior, because it's You . . .
Jesus, My Savior, because it's You . . .

A FATHER AND SO MUCH MORE...

...FIRST
You are their son, and they are very proud
to point you out from amid the crowd.
Your life is founded on what God has done,
and you share the love of His only Son

...AND
You are a husband, dad, and son-in-law.
You love, and comfort, and help with awe.
Our life together is based on God's grace,
and together, show that in every case.

...BETTER
You are a father to children you love.
They are precious gifts from God above.
You give them guidance, love, and care each day,
and you share their interests along the way.

...BEST
You are a father, the teacher all need.
All can see God's love in you, indeed.
As father, you are still one of God's best.
With you in our family, we are so blessed.

JUST A DREAM

I awoke, and I remembered the dream I had last night.
Emotions gripped my heart then.
I felt joy, but I was sad.
There was such lovely singing.
It made my heart rejoice . . .
In my ears was ringing,
the sound of my Father's voice!

Come in, my child, come in.
You have come home.
Let me dry your tears and take away your pain.
You have given much for me.
You suffered in my name.
Welcome home, child.
You are finally here.
Now live with me eternally,
and never shed a tear.

I was glad, then I remembered that man I saw last night.
He did not know the Savior.
Jesus' name, he'd never called.
My heart could not keep singing.
He seemed to know his fate . . .
In his ears came ringing
the words that he was too late!

Depart from me, depart.
What is your name?
You pretended love and church was just a game.
Sin was often fun for you.
You never felt the shame.
You must leave here.
You can't ever stay.
Now, live alone eternally.
There's nothing left to say.

I'm relieved, and I am thankful it was a dream last night.
I have more time to tell of
Jesus Christ, God's only Son.
He shed His blood to save us
from all our filthy sins.
In my ears, it's ringing
the song of His love begins.

Come in, my child, come in.
You're welcome here.
Now live with me eternally,
and never shed a tear.

Come in, my child, come in.
You're welcome here.
Now live with me eternally,
and never shed a tear.

CHOOSE JESUS

Take a look around your life.
Tell me what you see.
Do you have a future?
Are you living free?
Perhaps you haven't seen the time
you had to make a choice.
Will you choose to follow them,
or listen to another voice?

Make a vow unto yourself.
Let the whole world see.
Make a choice for yourself.
Be the best that you can be.
Be sure you know what you're doing.
Stand up and shout it out loud.
Know where your life is going.
Choose to know Jesus, be proud.

Take a look around your life.
Tell me what you see.
Can you see the future,
where you're living free?
Perhaps you know that He loves you.
He gave His life for all.
Will you listen to the world,
or listen to our Savior's call?

Make a vow to yourself.
Let the whole world see.
Make a choice for yourself.
Be the best that you can be.
Be sure you know what you're doing.
Stand up and shout it out loud.
Know where your life is going.
Choose to know Jesus, be proud.

You are a special person.
Take a look inside your heart, and see what I can see.
You are a special person.
So, take a step . . .
Choose Jesus, and be free.

I CAN CALL YOU LORD

This world possessed me.
It tried to keep me from Your light.
And all the time, life seemed to rhyme.
Sometimes, it even turned out right.
Still, my life was dark as night!
Even then,
I felt You there.
I knew You always cared.

Your pow'r was greater,
than this world's strongest hold on me.
You sent Your Son to be the One
to bleed and die on Calvary.
Now, new daylight sets me free.
Evermore,
my Savior lives.
His strength He always gives.

So . . .

Jesus, my Lord Jesus,
now, I can call You Lord.
By Your Holy Spirit's pow'r,
and by Your precious love each hour,
I've giv'n my heart to You.

Jesus, my Lord Jesus,
Yes, I can call You Lord.
By You bearing all my shame,
and by Your precious, holy name,
I've put my trust in You.

Jesus, my Lord Jesus,
yes, I can call You Lord.

Jesus, my Lord Jesus,
yes, I will call You Lord!

I'VE GOT THE VICTORY!

God allowed His Son
to die upon a cross.
But Jesus conquered death.
He has paid for all our sin.
Satan's battle has been lost!

Yes, it's been a while,
since Jesus gave His life.
But still, His blood gives grace
in each day I live for Him,
whether I find joy or strife.

I've got the victory,
The devil is defeated.
I've got the victory,
'Cause Jesus Christ is seated
at the right hand of God,
and the battle has been won!

So, the vict'ry's mine,
The war's already won,
and I can claim God's strength,
in my battles every day.
I don't ever have to run!

I've got the victory,
The devil is defeated.
I've got the victory,
'Cause Jesus Christ is seated
at the right hand of God,
and the battle has been won!

So, His vict'ry's mine,
and it can be yours, too!
And I can have God's pow'r
as I live for Him each day.
My dear friend, yes, so can you!

Just ask . . .

HIS NAME WAS JESUS

Light;
a special light
to announce a baby's birth.
It was a sign from God
that His Son had come to earth.
A brilliant star that shone so bright
foretold this dark world's purest light.
That eastern star, for a baby king,
brought joy to make all heaven sing.
Light;
a special light.
His name was Jesus.

Son;
God's only Son.
He would save the world from sin.
It was a gift from God
that salvation came for men.
A virgin's child, this Holy Son
became this dark world's promised one.
That precious child, yes, the baby king
brought peace that only God could bring.
Son;
God's only Son.
His name was Jesus.

Love;
a priceless love
to show us the Father's plan.
It was a sign from Him
that His Son would be a man.
A precious love, this one so dear,
became one of us living here.
Our Lord of love, yes, our Savior king

brought grace that only God could bring
Love;
a priceless love.
His name is Jesus.

NEW LIFE HAS JUST BEGUN

You think my life is dull.
Your judgement has been made.
You haven't given me a chance.
You've cast the part I've played.
But listen, friend.
Comprehend.
It's far from the end when you give yourself to Christ.
New life will just begin!

We have fun too.
Life is not a drag.
We love to smile and laugh,
when things begin to lag.
Each day is a new adventure.
Each day is a joyful song.
Each day is a bright beginning,
laughing, loving, growing strong!

You think I have no friends.
That's where you're really wrong
Because the friends I have are true.
They last a lifetime long.
So, listen now.
Find out how.
You can see right now if you give your life to Christ.
New life will just begin!

We have fun too.
Life is not a drag.
We love to smile and laugh,
when things begin to lag.
Each day is a new adventure.
Each day is a joyful song.
Each day is a bright beginning,
laughing, loving, growing strong!

GOD'S GIFT

God has given us our family by blood.
He gave a precious Mother and Dad.
This family includes many others,
Maybe brothers, sisters, cousins we had.

Nothing can compare to special grandparents.
That's what I think, and what about you?
Do you have a special aunt or uncle?
All family no matter what we do.

God gave to me the very best Mom and Dad.
Because of them, I have been so blessed.
He gave me two brothers to share for life.
Growing up with them was the very best.

You never know what children that God will give.
Maybe boys or girls, or maybe each.
I love the two brothers that God gave me,
But I had no sister, who I could reach.

As the years have passed by, God has shown me now.
Through my brothers' marriages of love
He's gifted the answer I could not reach.
You, two precious sisters to me through love.

THE WORDS TO SAY

I see His love in something as brief as a raindrop,
Yet, it's love that is endless as eternity.
He's given me all His blessings and His love, it is true.
But not just to me, my friend.
He's given them to you!

It seems that you find refuge in the sin of the world,
But all those worldly friends are not real friends at all.
You see the black of the night, but not the true light of day.
But Jesus is truth, my friend.
He'll guide you on your way!

If you can't see His love or don't know that He's caring.
Though it's filled up with sin, your life's an empty place.
He'll come into your heart, and He'll open your eyes for sure.
And He'll let you see, my friend,
He'll love you evermore!

A VERY SPECIAL DAY

It was a very special day.
The family and the world were so blessed.
It's still a very special day.
We need to celebrate it to the best!

The Father gave a precious boy,
to grow and learn, and become a young man.
He was meant to bring precious joy,
as God teaches us daily that we can!

This precious boy became that man.
From God, and parents, and his teachers too,
he learned and grew to have a plan,
showing everyone all that they could do!

He is a very special man,
son and brother, husband, dad and grandpa,
A man who loves Jesus Christ, and
a man who worships our God with much awe!

It was a very special day
when our precious Father gave him his birth.
We celebrate this special day.
God's gift of life filled with His Holy worth!

Happy Birthday with love!

A MOMENT'S PRAYER

All my thoughts . . . my dreams . . . my emotions . . .
I place them in Your hands.
Take me
and
use me,
Father, I pray,
to comfort a neighbor, to share with the lost;
to give where there is a need.
Make me Your servant.
Show me the way.
I want to follow Your lead.

All the days . . . the weeks . . . the long hard years . . .
I know You're by my side.
Comfort
and
strengthen,
Father, I pray,
to carry the burden, to bear earthly pain;
to see when I lose my way.
You are my Father
You are my friend.
I need You there every day.

GO

In Jerusalem . . . in our neighborhoods.
To Judea . . . to the folks nearby.
In Samaria . . . across the land.
To the ends of the earth . . . into all the world.

Go into all the world and teach.
Go into all the world and preach;
making disciples and telling of His love.
Tell of His mercy, sent from above.
Tell all the people you may see,
Christ lived and died and rose to life,
so we could all be free.

For . . .

When the Spirit is in you,
His power comes to stay.
Just ask Him for the words you need.
He'll tell you what to say.
He will give you strength
to witness for your Lord.
For we are missionaries, all in one accord.

Go in the Spirit's pow'r and share.
Go in the Spirit's pow'r and care
Share His forgiveness and showing His great joy.
Share of His sweet peace, none can destroy.
Tell everyone you see each day,
Christ left His throne, and came to earth,
to bring a better way.

For . . .

When the Spirit is in you,
His power comes to stay.
Just ask Him for the words you need.
He'll tell you what to say.
He will give you strength
to witness for your Lord.
For we are missionaries, all in one accord.

IN EVERYTHING GIVE THANKS

As I look around me, questions fill my mind.
Scoffers laugh, and people say, "I thought your God was kind".

So, I ask . . .

"Why did she die, Oh Lord?
She was just a little child.
Why is she gone, dear Lord?
She just lived a little while.
Tell me why is there hunger,
And why so much pain?
Father, what is the purpose?
Is it all in vain?"

"Why is there hate, Oh Lord
I can't seem to understand.
Why can't we love, dear Lord,
And reach out for someone's hand.
Tell me, why is there killing,
And why so much fear?
Father, what is the reason?
Are you really near?"

As I wait for answers, His peace fills me here.
His Word speaks with love and care, "My child, don't ever fear."

In everything, give thanks, My child.
For you, this is My will.
You cannot understand it all,
But trust Me, and be still.

IN YOUR WAY

I see the sunrise.
The day is new.
I lift my voice Lord, in praise to You.
I feel the warmth of Your care.
I know You're with me everywhere.
All Your goodness, I must share with those I meet.

I know You're here, God.
To You I yield.
I thank You Father, for You are real.
You give Your strength when I'm weak.
You lead me as Your will I seek.
In my spirit, I feel peace as I praise You.

I see Your children,
Live in defeat.
I share Your love, God, with those I meet.
I know our life is Your Son.
In Him, the war's already won.
All Your mercy, You do give to all for free.

I worship Father,
My heart renews.
I thank You Jesus for all You do.
I feel Your strength when I fail.
You protect me when the storms rail.
All Your love holds me through sorrow and through pain.

Oh Lord, please live Your life through me.
Shine through me every day.
Every moment, help me stay . . .
Walking . . . talking . . . loving . . .
In Your way!

LOVE

Love . . . it was a man.
Love . . . it was God's plan.
Love brought Jesus Christ down to the earth.
Love . . . in human form, as a baby born.
Love brought Jesus Christ down to the earth.

Only He could leave His glory.
Only He could die.
Only He could pay the debt I owe for all my sin.
He was the perfect Lamb.
He is "the Great I Am".
Only Christ could take my place and die for me to live.

Love . . . it was a cross.
Love . . . is what it cost.
Love raised Jesus Christ up from the grave.
Love . . . was victory, won for you and me.
Love raised Jesus Christ up from the grave.

Only He could leave His glory.
Only He could die.
Only He could pay the debt I owe for all my sin.
He was the perfect Lamb.
He is "the Great I Am".
Only Christ could take my place and die for me to live.

Love . . . is what I bring.
Love . . . is Christ my king.
Love is Jesus Christ who lives in me.
Love . . . to seek and share with all those I meet
Love is Jesus Christ who lives in me.

Only He could leave His glory.
Only He could die.
Only He could pay the debt I owe for all my sin.
He was the perfect Lamb.
He is "the Great I Am".
Only Christ could take my place and die for me to live.

MERCY, GRACE AND LOVE

God's mercy, His grace and love,
are offered to us all from above.
They are giv'n without a fee.
We only need to accept; they're free!

His Son paid our price for sin,
when He gave His life so all could win
Just believe in Jesus Christ.
Know He sacrificed to pay our price!

In sin, we each deserve death.
We aren't entitled to our next breath,
yet God has blessed with His grace.
So, trust that Jesus did take our place!

Live your life, share what you know
to all those you meet, let His love show.
Tell them of the mercy shown,
when we accept from our God alone!

NOT ONE FATHER, BUT TWO!
A DAUGHTER'S TRIBUTE

My father was a special man;
a giant among men.
He gave himself for all of us,
then gave more love again.
He was gentle, steadfast, kind and strong.
With pride, and courage, and love for life,
He quietly suffered long.

I loved my father,
and I always will.
He was one of the best,
But God said he should come to be with Him,
in perfect joy and rest.
Sometimes God's purpose seems strange to us.
We often cannot see.
Still, I thank God, He only knows and does what's best,
for all, not only me.

God has for each a perfect plan;
so special and so good.
He gave another father then,
as only my God could.
He was quiet, thoughtful, kind and true.
With strength and caring, he gave his love,
as only fathers do.

I loved this father,
and I always will.
He ranks in the top few,
and though I still don't understand it all,
I know one thing is true.
God's special blessings and more are mine,
because of Dad and you.
And I thank God, He's given me such special gifts;
not one father, but two.

LORD JESUS

Lord Jesus, I know you died.
It was for my sin you were crucified.
I can't wait another moment.
My heart I give right now.
Come into my life and live through me.
I give to you my vow.

Lord Jesus, I've lived in sin,
but, on the cross, You were able to win.
I have found the only answer.
My life has been made new.
Come into my heart and love through me,
in all I ever do.

Lord Jesus, You are divine.
Let me show the world as God's glory shines
Since I've found the only answer
a gift to me that's free.
Come into my heart and share through me,
with everyone I see.

YOU ARE WORTHY

Jesus,
see the little child.
Jesus,
she's so meek and mild.
She is unworthy of Your love.

Jesus,
See that lonely man.
Jesus,
with old, withered hands.
He is unworthy of Your love.

Still, you give them all Your purest love.
On the cross, Your life for them You gave.
God's price for sin was paid.
Jesus, You are so worthy of their love!

Jesus,
I am sorrow-filled.
Jesus,
help me know Your will.
I am unworthy of Your love.

Jesus,
There is trouble here.
Jesus,
in Your world so dear.
We are unworthy of Your love.

Still, You give us all Your purest love.
On the cross, Your life for us You gave.
Our price for sin was paid.
Jesus, You are so worthy of our love.

Jesus, You are so worthy of our love!

JESUS, HOLY ONE

Jesus, Holy One;
One in God, His own Son.
Glory, honor, and praise to thee,
ever from my lips shall be.
You made the sun, the sky, the sea.
How infinite your pow'r must be.

But You love me, so weak, so small.
Yes, You love me.
You love us all.
It's hard for me to understand,
but that great love brought You to man.

Jesus, Holy one;
One in God, His own Son.
You came, You lived, and died for me,
to show grace You have for me.
You sacrificed so all can see,
how precious is Your love for me.

But You love me, so weak, so small.
Yes, You love me.
You love us all.
It's hard for me to understand,
but that great love brought You to man.

Jesus, Holy One;
One in God, His own Son.
You share Your love with me each day.
You listen and hear me pray.
You share the Father's love and say
that every day You'll show the way.

A SPECIAL LADY

Mom Mom, Granny, Mom Mom Mom,
Grandmother, Great grandmother, too.
Lula, Lizzie, or Miss Lu.
Which one was she to you?

It really doesn't matter
which special name that you held dear.
For one who lived a full life
and touched so many here.

Some lived close by; down the street,
'cross town, or just houses apart.
Others lived so far away,
still, she was in each heart.

All our memories can't be shared
in moments we have here today,
but let me tell you a few.
Hold tight to what I say.

So young at heart she has been.
She sat with the kids on the floor,
reading, puzzles, playing games
Yahtzee, Scrabble and War.

The birds would come; she loved them,
at the beach or in the side yard.
A joy was hers to feed them
with bread and biscuits hard.

She loved the Lord and His Word.
She taught it to children back then.
Through rough times and good times too,
her faith in God has been.

Memories of this one so dear,
are for us who miss her and grieve.
Rejoice, for she has found peace,
and joy she'll never leave.

Activities

LITTLE BITS OF LOVE AND FUN TO SHARE

Our lives are made up of smaller periods of time . . . hours, days, weeks, months, years, etc. The "little bits" that follow are for just that! They are ideas, activities, and fun things you can fit into small amounts of time. Most of them have been tried and tested with very special results. Read through them, and decide which would be appropriate for your child/children. One may not fit with their current age, but would be perfect in a few months. Some may work better with your elementary child rather than a preschooler. Whichever fun things and activities you choose, you'll find that it only takes a little effort to spend good quality time with your children. That effort will multiply and mean much to them now and as they grow. As I've said it over and over again, life is so short. They'll grow up before you know it. Each day is precious because you're alive and together as a family.

As you pray, and seek God's will, I know you will find a couple that can become meaningful to you and your family. Continue to pray and seek God's will. I know He will bless you with other "little bits" especially for you and your family. As you and your family spend these "little bits" of time together, use them to memorize short Bible verses that are used with the activities.

A PICNIC

Take your children on a picnic! Everyone does it in the story books and movies, so why not in real life. Fix a lunch, pile your little ones in the car, and find a spot near your home. A park with a playground and tables under shady trees is a good location, but not absolutely necessary for a successful picnic. Check around the area where you live. With a soft blanket, you can make a perfect picnic spot by a lake, in a park, at the beach or maybe even at the zoo!

When you begin to plan for your picnic, you might think of the traditional basket filled with fried chicken, potato salad and all the fixin's. That could be just a little too much for you… just enough work to say, "forget it"! (I've had that thought before!) Don't worry. Children are usually happier with something simple like peanut butter and jelly sandwiches, chips and cookies. They may like to pick the menu and help you prepare something even better. You can take a thermos of milk or juice, or pick up little cartons along the way. With a little effort and thought, you're on your way to lots of love and loads of fun. (If you find there's no park or lake close to your home, just have it in your own backyard. That will be just as much fun, and perhaps a little easier to pull off!)

You can stop there and still have fun. Sure, you can gobble up the great food and enjoy the fresh air. But, when you've come this far, why not add something extra? See what your imagination can do! Make up a situation and act it out. You'll probably find that your precious children can help with the pretending. Think of another setting; the beach, the mountains, at a campfire. Talk about what you might see or do. Who knows, you could all pretend to be on a surfboard, catching a wave!

A way to double the fun is to plan your picnic for the weekend or on Dad's day off. Another idea is to take your picnic to Dad's office for lunch, so he can share in the good time for a while. (Don't forget to check this out with him first!)

What about a rainy or snowy day? That doesn't mean you can't have a sunny day inside the house! Instead of just a regular lunch at the table or counter, change the setting and have a picnic on your kitchen or family room floor. Spread your blanket, munch on your lunch, and then play some games, sing songs, or act out a little play. Before you know it, those raindrops or snowflakes on the outside will turn into laughter on the inside!

BIRTHDAYS

At our house, birthdays have always been a "Big Deal"!! Some folks exchange cards, while others give gifts. We've always had some kind of party to commemorate the special day. Sometimes, we like to make it a week-long family celebration. Look for ways that you and your children can bring joy to your family and friends around you.

It's the thought that counts. You can brighten someone's day without a lot of fuss or expense. With a little bit of effort, you and your children can use a birthday to provide a fun family activity to share. It's so easy to stop at the store to pick up a birthday card for Grandma. With the children, it can definitely be more fun to make one for her. It could be six inches or six feet tall, or anywhere in between! Take a piece of construction paper or poster board, and fold it in half to make a giant greeting card for the special birthday person. Help the children plan a design for the front. Visit the craft store near you to find construction paper, glue, glitter, etc. If one of your children is old enough to write, guide them on where to put the "Happy Birthday" greeting. Or, why not let each child make one of their own to share? Give them construction paper, crayons, markers, glue, etc., and maybe a little or a lot of guidance (depending on the age of your artists). I really think Grandma (or anyone) would enjoy the artwork of that special child much more than something from the card section. You could even make a cake, and let the children help decorate and deliver it.

Sing "Happy Birthday" to a friend down the street or a relative 500 miles away. Take a friend of the family, or family member for a birthday (or any day) surprise. Invite them to go for a quick shopping trip to the bookstore, mall or somewhere close by. On the way home, pull into the parking lot of a restaurant that prepares delicious pies, cakes or milkshakes. You (and your children) can shout "Surprise"! Whether the friend's birthday was last week, today, or next week, it doesn't matter. Just tell them that you wanted to give a surprise to them as a special birthday treat. (This idea can also be used for any other reason for a surprise celebration.)

HOUSEWORK

You might think that children and housework do not go together. I'll admit, there are days when the best place for your youngsters is to be out in the yard or in their room, away from what you're doing. If your husband calls to say his boss is coming home with him for dinner, and the house looks like a tornado just swept through, then head the children toward the swing set and sandbox. Another excellent example is when you will be using highly toxic preparations or dangerous tools. These are times when little ones should be kept at a safe distance from where you are working. First, and foremost, use logic and common sense in any activity you share with your children. Don't ever take a chance with their safety, when you have the slightest question in your mind.

Teaching Time

On days when you aren't hurrying to meet a deadline, or using dangerous chemicals or tools, general house cleaning can be fun with a helper by your side. It is especially rewarding to include a preschooler in activities of your day while older brothers or sisters are at school. The time will pass more quickly for both of you if they help you change the sheets, make the beds, dust, pick up and vacuum, etc. Depending on the child's age, you can determine how much independence you can give them. Of course, you'll be right there while they are learning. Some jobs may require a close eye all the time, while others can get by with an occasional check.

Whenever we work together, we spend part of the time singing. Again, this keeps both you and your "little assistant" from getting bored. Both of my girls beam with pride when I sing "The Helper Song" (one of the Prayer and Praise, Love and Fun songs). I always use this when it's time to pick up toys or clean their room, or any time they help. I think they feel as though they've really been a great help to Mommy or Daddy . . . and they have!

I've found that my children have days when they want to stay at it until I finish. On other days, they decide they'd rather be outside or in their playroom after the first job is finished. Staying flexible and patient is always helpful. Sometimes one particular task interests a child. My girls have always enjoyed dusting and drying the silverware. Little boys might enjoy learning to sweep the walk after daddy mows the lawn. It might be more fun for them to be outside helping to wash the family car. You never know . . . the girls may like to do those things as well.

When you begin, take the time to demonstrate, and allow for practice. Don't forget to give lots of encouragement and praise. After a while, your children will be able to do many "little jobs" unassisted. At the same time, they're helping Mommy and Daddy, they are learning to be clean, neat, and responsible children. This is important training time that should gradually develop into some specific daily habits. When children are old enough to be responsible for certain chores around the house, (like cleaning their own room) it won't be something foreign to them.

VALENTINE'S DAY

Valentine's Day is a happy, loving day! A fun activity to do together the week before would be making cards. I wouldn't recommend trying to make twenty for friends in a Sunday School class. That might take too much time and work. It would be nice to make them for family and a few very close friends. My girls and I spent two evenings making six cards for grandparents and close friends. It was worth every minute. They were so very happy with their pretty Valentines that I thought they would burst with pride!

Each one consisted of one piece of construction paper, some lacy hearts, and some pictures they cut out from magazines or coloring books. Each girl added her personal feelings on the inside. With the extra glue, the smears, and a few little scissor mistakes, I must say they were beautiful. I doubted that the recipients would consider trading them in for one of the largest and most expensive brands a card shop had to offer. (The secret comments I heard from all the recipients definitely confirmed my thoughts!)

EASTER

Make An Easter Centerpiece

This would be an activity for an elementary school-aged child who has attended Sunday School and learned the story of Jesus; how He came from God and was born in a manger, how He lived, and how he gave His life for all of us.

This activity will give you something to place in your home every Easter. You don't have to be a floral designer or a sculptor to make a meaningful centerpiece or table arrangement. Begin with a square piece of styrofoam. Cover it with moss, and secure with hair pins or glue. In one back corner, push a cross down into the Styrofoam, so it stands. (It can be made by gluing two small tree branches, or two pieces of wood in the shape of a cross.) Cut a rectangular piece of white fabric, drape it where the cross meets and glue it there. On the opposite back corner, mold an open cave with clay to represent the tomb where Jesus was buried. Fill in with a silk Easter lily bloom in front. (An artificial bloom could be used so it would last. If you like, you can make a figure of Jesus, standing by the lily. He could be made like the figures in the Christmas Nativity scene. (If you don't have the supplies for this project, you can find what you need at a craft store, or a large "multi-product" grocery store".) Another option would be to have your helper cut out a colored picture of Jesus from a Christmas coloring book. This could be glued to a stick and stuck into the Styrofoam.

Let your children help with the project. As you work, talk to them about what the Bible teaches us of the Easter story. You could even read the story to them of Jesus coming to earth and dying on the cross for us (sneaking in a reminder of His birth in the manger). Show them as you make the cross where He died, and then was put in the tomb. Tell them that God made Jesus alive again.

Share that Jesus lives with His Father now, but also knows us, helps us, and prays for us every day.

CHRISTMAS

It's November 26, and Christmas is a month away. Did you finish your Christmas shopping weeks ago, or are you like me? Have you just begun to think about your long list? Every year it seems the world becomes more and more commercialized. Santa Claus is placed high on a pedestal (on every street corner and in every mall) for all the world to see. If you keep your eyes and ears open, you'll see him and hear the jolly music earlier and earlier every year!

With all the commercial noise beginning, Jesus is tucked under the tree behind all the presents. Many, many children don't even know who He is or why He's there. You can, and you must make Christmas a very special time in your home as you celebrate the birth of Jesus Christ. You must make sure your children know that without Jesus, there truly is no Christmas! I hope you select from these ideas to begin or add to your own family traditions.

A Personal Touch

Most children love to color. Even preschoolers enjoy spreading bright colors across the page to create their own little "masterpieces". Look for a coloring book that depicts the Christmas Story. A bookstore is a great place to find these. If you are unable to find one, use another kind with happy pictures.

Share the idea with your children so they can get excited about contributing their talents. Have them color a picture each day during December. Talk about the scene in the Christmas Story they are coloring. Try to make the story of Jesus' birth come alive for them as they color. Store the pictures in a special place when they finish. The idea you shared with your children will then make gift giving more personal and very special. When you wrap your gifts for family and friends, roll up a colored picture and tie it with a ribbon. Then tape it to the top of the gift. Grandma and Grandpa will love the addition to the beautiful gift wrap. The personalized picture will surely be displayed on their refrigerator when they return home. When a non-Christian receives a gift with this special touch from your family, it will be a witness to them. With the trend toward crafts and homemade gifts, everyone will appreciate this extra touch, especially when it's filled with love from a child. The activity will be a wonderful way to teach and reinforce your children's knowledge of the Christmas Story. Coloring time can be used as a conclusion to your devotion time, or as a fun activity at another time during the day.

Make Your Family Nativity Scene

Children love to make things with paper, glue, and crayons, especially when you are there to help and share in the fun. You can look for a "how-to" craft ideas book at a Christian book store or a craft store. As the project may take a few days, use the time to talk about the birth of the baby Jesus with your children. You can also make it a month-long project by working on it a little each day.

A gift box or shoe box makes a perfect stable when standing on its side, and covered with pine straw or hay that's been glued on. (I've found that a box that held men's shoes or boots tends to be a good choice.) You can follow step-by-step instructions in a book to make the characters, or design your own with odds and ends you have around the house. Old-fashioned clothespins with pipe cleaner arms and faces drawn on the end can make great bodies. Cut a simple rectangle of fabric and glue onto the body to create a robe. Cotton balls or batting can be glued on as hair and beards. To give the hair color, use a gray or black marker. Heavy cardboard glued to a clump of modeling clay will provide a stand to set each of your characters in.

Your ideas may be much more interesting and artistic than mine. However, if you feel you have no creative bones in your body, find an inexpensive children's storybook or coloring book. You can cut out the characters and the animals and let your children glue them to a piece of cardboard or poster board that is folded to stand up. This is good for the very young children who don't use scissors yet. The older ones can cut out the characters themselves and glue them on. The Bible characters can be as simple or complicated as you and your children want them to be. The important thing is that it is a beautiful picture of you and your family sharing the story of Jesus' coming to us in a manger. No matter how you decide to construct your own nativity scene, it can be something you will use and cherish for years to come. What a precious scene for friends and family to see under your tree. I'm sure your children will have something to share with them about its creation.

When you carefully wrap those lights and ornaments from your tree, make a special effort to store the nativity carefully. Wrap each character and the stable in tissue paper, and place them inside a tightly sealed bag. The extra gift you give your family by creating a homemade nativity together will be well worth the effort. It can become a very special part of your Christmas traditions.

Visit Someone

Share your love and your lives with someone who will be alone on the holidays. Check with your church. They may be able to point you in the direction of a special member who has no family. Visit a nursing home to brighten the day of an elderly person. You and your children can take a gift (something bought, or better yet, made or baked by your family). A paper Christmas tree or any other decoration delivered to those at the nursing home by you and your children would mean so much. Make sure to include some of the personalized Christmas pictures that have been colored by your children. Perhaps you could even share a Christmas carol with them.

Make A Birthday Cake For Jesus!

Much of the world at this time of year is full of shopping and Santa. This is a beautiful way to share the real reason for Christmas with your children. You could start with either a Christmas Bible story or reading scripture with them. Depending on their age, you can decide the best way to handle this fun activity. If you're not a baker with your own special cake recipe, just pick a delicious box mix from the store. Your children can help with stirring the ingredients and anything that is appropriate for their age. If they are old enough, they can frost the cake. Perhaps make one for each child to decorate. Elementary-aged children would probably love to watch you, and follow by decorating one of their own. You could purchase the letters to put on top of the cake in the bakery aisle to spell out "Happy Birthday Jesus". It's a great idea to take photographs while sharing this activity. Grandparents would love to receive pictures of their precious grandchildren participating and learning. What a special Christmas keepsake to have of them wishing the Lord Jesus Happy Birthday!

Make Your Own Greeting Cards

As with some of the other activities, this can be done using pictures from a coloring book with scenes from Jesus' birth. Your children can color the pictures, cut them out and glue them on a piece of folded construction paper. Those who are old enough to print can write a message on the inside area, and add a "Merry Christmas" to the front with the picture. If they are able, or if they prefer, children might want to color their own picture on the front. I'm sure relatives and friends would love to receive a Christmas card from your family. How often do they receive a special card like this that has been created by such a famous artist?

A WALK

It's a beautiful spring, summer or fall day. The children are begging you to take them for a walk to the park that's a few blocks away. You're up to your elbows in laundry and other daily chores. Feeling a little guilty, you hurry them out the door and down the street. Once the half-hour limit (that you set) on their play time is reached, you rush them back to their own fenced yard. You say to yourself, "We all got some fresh air and exercise. Now I must get busy." Sometimes, it's absolutely necessary to do it this way! Sometimes, this may be all we feel like doing. If this is your style all the time, maybe you should back up and think about your priorities. Our most important task as a mother is to raise our children in the best way we possibly can. There's so much more a "creative, God-inspired mother" can do with a walk around the block or a visit to the park.

Praise Time

You can accomplish so many things at once, if you make a walk with your children a *Praise Time*. First, tell them that something special is coming up, as you prepare to leave the house. If you build up your activities, and give them a special name, it might produce new enthusiasm and excitement. An experience that has been rushed, boring, or "yucky" in the past, will become an exciting, fun time that your children (and you) will look forward to. Once you are out the door, and on your way, announce that "Today's walk is going to be a *Praise Time*. We're going to praise God for everything we see on our walk!" (Don't forget to plan some of these special walks for the weekends, when Dad can come along.)

What an opportunity to encourage and teach the Word of God to your children. I Thessalonians says, "In everything give thanks; for this is God's will for you in Christ Jesus." You can take the time during a walk to thank God, and praise Him for the things you see. A time like a walk can begin the practice if you or your children have never known this lesson God teaches. If you already know it is something you should do, this can be one way to reinforce thanksgiving and praise in the life of your family. Everyone can benefit from a refresher in the concept that all of our thoughts in our minds and the attitudes in our hearts are part of "praying without ceasing". Your family *Praise Time* walk can be the beginning of a victorious life of continuous praise to the Lord. I know you and your children will discover things around your home and neighborhood in a way that you have never seen before.

Add a fun dimension to your praise, by making it a game. As you spot something special, call it out. "Look at the pretty yellow crocus coming up! I thank God for making the pretty flowers."

"There's a little squirrel running across the fence. Praise you God for the animals." At the park, siblings might watch each other on a swing or a slide. That might give them the chance to say "praise you God for my little sister". See who can find the most things to praise God for. No matter how varied your children's ages, you can adapt this activity to fit. Make it easier for the little ones, and add a few extra requirements for older children. As well as getting fresh air and exercise that's important for you and your children, you've learned more about the world God has created. You've blessed the Lord with your praise, and He has blessed your obedience to His Word. You have spent important time with your children; loving them, teaching them, and giving them your attention and love.

"God Made Me" Time

This can be done at other times, and almost anywhere, but it's fun when incorporated into a walk around the block. Preschoolers and elementary school children hear in Sunday School that God created them; He made them. This activity can help them become more aware of the miracle of the creation called our human body. It's like "follow the leader" with an extra twist! As you're walking along, and you come to a crack in the sidewalk, you might say, "God made me with two feet, so I can jump over this crack. How about you?" Each child gets to say this to the next person, and then jumps over the crack. Everyone tries to think of something they can do, because of the way God has made us.

Examples: "God made me with two hands, so I can clap!" "God made me with a nose to smell, so I can smell these flowers." This can be a way to make physical exercise fun. "God made me with two strong legs, so I can run to that tree. How about you?"

<u>Time To Sing</u>

This is one of my favorite things to do anytime. If you like, you and your children can make up songs about nature or people you see on your walk. If that's not your specialty, sing songs you learned growing up. My children love to sing songs they learn in Sunday School. There are several short songs in the last part of this book that are very simple to learn and sing. Learn one or two to suit your children's personalities or needs; or maybe you can use all of them. Music is soothing, and it can be a lot of fun. Even the little ones can hum along if they don't know the words. Through repetition, they'll pick up a few words each time. A song can make the same scenery we saw yesterday and the day before, appear new. A song can put sunshine back into a cloudy sky.

Singing can take a half hour ride to the doctor's office or shopping and cut it down to almost no time at all. The next time your little ones are fussing in the back seat, try having a "time to sing". See how many different songs you can sing before you arrive at your destination. Their fussing might become shouts of praise to their Heavenly Father. They also might find out that Mommy (or Daddy) is a lot of fun to be with when it's time to sing. Don't forget that if everyone is singing, it's difficult to fuss.

Often, singing as you walk or ride down the street with your children, can open the door to be a witness to those in your neighborhood. You never know who might be listening. We're always getting smiles from people sitting next to us at stoplights. Perhaps you'll brighten up someone's day! Don't ever worry if you don't have a beautiful voice. God told us to make a joyful noise unto the Lord. Just lift your voice in song and praise to Him with your children. He will use it.

<u>Monthly Walk Around the Bookstore</u>

We love going to big bookstores like Barnes & Noble. They have books for every child of any age. Some stores have a special storytelling time for groups of children. They have a section that features Christian storybooks. Not only do they carry books, but you can find all kinds of toys, games, music and other activities to use as a family. Making a trip to get a new book each month is a fun outing, no matter how old your child is. It can be an activity you all will look forward to. Topping off your bookstore visit with some ice cream at the shop down the street could make this monthly occasion even more special.

Songs of Prayer, Praise, Love and Fun

Who says a baby is too young to praise God? They may not be able to sing along yet, but they can listen to older brothers and sisters. They will be able to share songs they've learned in Sunday School. If they are the first child in the family, they can share this time with Mommy and Daddy. As soon as they can, you'll find them joining in worship with you.

Many people have a stereotyped concept of what prayer and praise are supposed to be. They believe you must be on your knees, or sitting in a pew, with hands folded and eyes closed to pray. They agree that singing hymns or worship choruses, with your hands held high in surrender to the Lord is another way to praise the Lord. Yes, I agree! These are definitely ways to worship and praise our God, but the Bible tells us to "pray without ceasing" in I Thessalonians 4:17. What about I Thessalonians 5:18, "In everything give thanks for this is the will of God in Christ Jesus". If we are to obey God's Word, we must be in a manner or attitude of prayer and praise all the time. What better way to begin teaching this truth to our babies, preschoolers and elementary age children than having fun with music and words they can understand.

Share Love and Fun in a Quick Song

This section includes original short songs and choruses. Each has a simple melody line that can be sung. They can also be fun to recite as poems. All songs can be used by parents with their preschool through elementary age children. Many correspond with different activities they participate in during the day. Others are just nice or fun to sing or recite.

I've used these songs with my preschool daughters, and they love them. They give me an opportunity to show them attention and love. Sometimes they give us a chance to giggle together and give hugs. Others help teach a lesson or help them learn how to give God the praise He deserves every day.

Everyone needs to know that they are loved. It has been proven that children need to know this. It is essential for them to grow into healthy adults. We all want to be recognized for our accomplishments, whether big or small. It makes us feel good about ourselves. This builds our self-esteem and confidence. If we, as parents, fail to let our children know we love them, we're proud of them, and we have confidence in them, they'll have little self-esteem as teens and adults. Our lack of positive reinforcement and sharing our deep love may be responsible for our children's failure someday.

Some people have a hard time expressing their love by hugging or kissing, or even touching their children. This is so sad. Perhaps you have this difficulty in your family. One of these choruses might give you the opportunity to share your feelings with the babies, preschoolers, or elementary age children in your family. Maybe it's not you, but Dad or big brother who can't, or doesn't like to show his love. Some of the songs may seem silly. That's what they're meant to be. They are meant to be fun, to make everyone smile, and to make memories. If you share them with the family, they often catch on. They will be very important to the little ones in your home. You may say that you aren't a singer, or that you can't come close to carrying a tune. God makes it clear in the book of Psalms that we are to "Make a joyful noise!"

Begin singing (or reciting) these fun songs and "prayer and praise" songs with your children and your grandchildren. I know God will do wonderful things as you do.

Announcing Breakfast, Lunch, Dinner, or Snack Time

You can fuss or yell to your children, telling them to put down their toys when it's time for meals. Why not make it sound like what's coming up will be more fun? Substitute the items on your menu in the verse. Use different foods for each meal! Use one verse for the upcoming meal. (You can also fill in the word "snack", and use some healthy items to eat.) This might make you and your family smile all the way to the dinner table!

Come Eat

Always Give Positive Words of Encouragement

I was always looking for ways to encourage my children to learn. This song helped them to learn that picking up toys, or other chores could be fun. Giving a big hug and kiss are also positive, loving ways to praise them for helping. If they hear you praising them for "helping out", I can almost guarantee you'll get a smile! Giving a big squeeze and kiss on the cheek as you say the words will make it a very special song in your house. It's great for when your child is assisting you with chores around the house. Just change the name to that of your special assistant at the time!

Heather Is A Helper

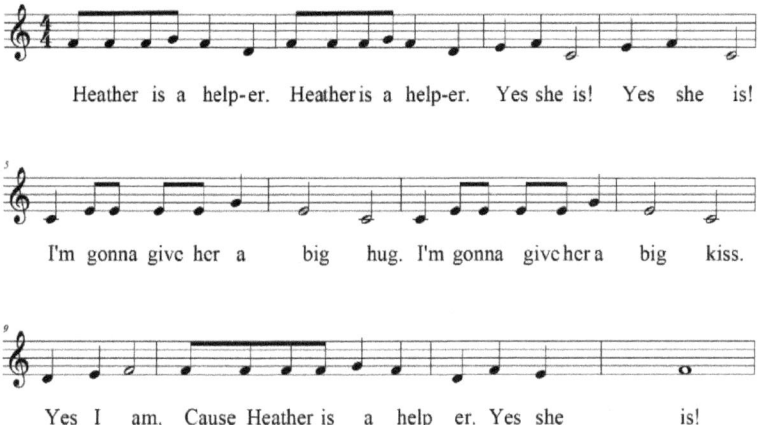

A Fun Way to Sing and Praise Jesus

If you're taking a walk, playing in the backyard, or at the park, you can use this little song to make everyone smile. One or two lines at a time might be a good start to learn the words. You can always add the next few and eventually sing the complete song together!

Hop! Hop! Hop!

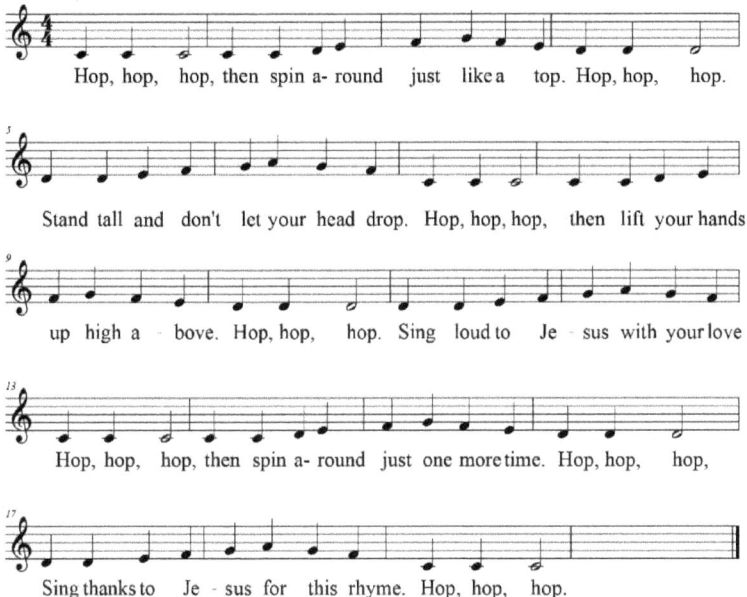

Show Them Special Love All the Time

This is a song or poem to be used anytime, all the time, and as often as possible. It's good to use when you tell your child that they've been a good helper. If your kindergartener or elementary student had a difficult day at school, they'll feel your love when you sing it to them. Just fill in your child's name. Also, this one should always be ended with a hug or two, or maybe three!

I Love You

Reminding Us of Our Special Friend

You can break this down and use one verse at a time to learn with the younger children. When they're ready and able, add another. It's a great one to sing or recite while riding in the car.

Jesus Is My Friend

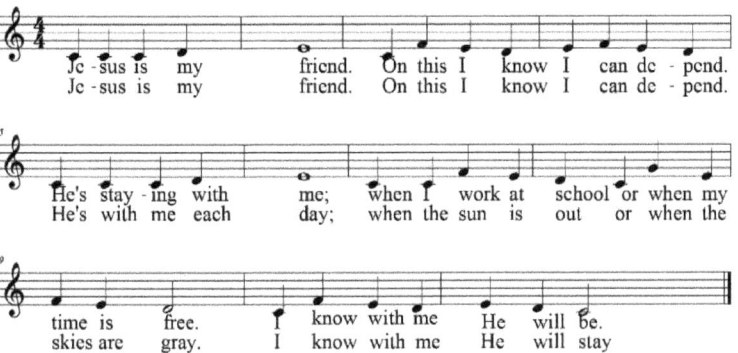

Sing a Song

Tickle You

A Fun Way to Wake Up

A song can be a fun way to get your children out of bed in the morning or after a nap. They will "almost" look forward to you coming in to wake them up!

Wake Up!

Finding Sunshine on a Not-So-Sunny Day

When a child looks out the window and sees rain or snow pouring down, it might bring tears or grouchiness inside. You can help show them that they can be content with the circumstances. Sing a song to bring out a smile or a laugh. Turn their complaining around in the opposite direction. It will be up to you set the words to the current weather and specific activity. (Use words like those in bold print to make your appropriate choices). Show them a "sunny" attitude, and let it rub off with a song!

(*Fill in any bad weather, like *"snowflakes"*, *"lightning"* or *"cold wind"*, etc.).

(fill in any activity like *"play a game"*, *"bake cookies"*, *"watch movies"*, *read a book,* etc.)**

Whatever the Weather

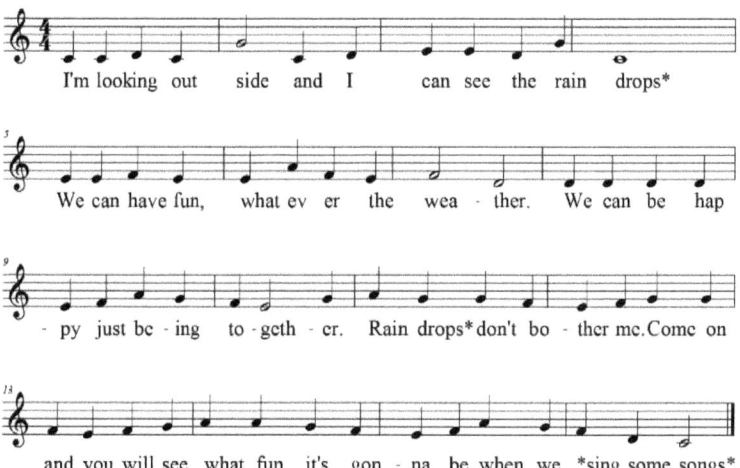

God Has Blessed our World with So Much

The trees, the sun, and the birds are just the tip of the iceberg. Use this when you're taking a walk, playing in the backyard, or making a visit to the park. When you're outside with your children, you can sing this song. It can also be a catalyst to start a conversation with them about other things they see that God made. Once they learn the song, let them pick something to fill in one of the items already there. It can be a continuing learning experience about the amazing creation we were given.

God Made So Much For Us

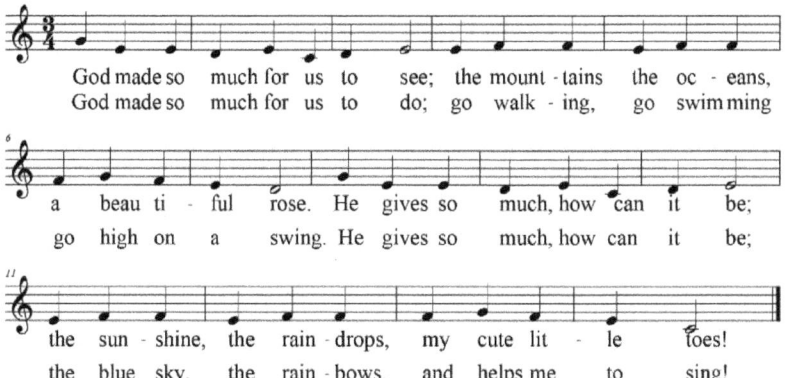

God made so much for us to see; the mount-tains the oc-eans,
God made so much for us to do; go walk-ing, go swim ming

a beau-ti-ful rose. He gives so much, how can it be;
go high on a swing. He gives so much, how can it be;

the sun-shine, the rain-drops, my cute lit-tle toes!
the blue sky, the rain-bows, and helps me to sing!

God Made All Things

www.ingramcontent.com/pod-product-compliance
Lightning Source LLC
Chambersburg PA
CBHW061220070526
44584CB00029B/3909